A PLACE FOR YOU

Reflections on Heaven

Jon Courson

Preface

It has been said that a person can be so heavenly-minded that he's no earthly good, but I have found that you can really be of little earthly good until you are heavenly-minded! For only when we have the eternal perspective and blessed hope of Heaven will we be able to navigate through life's inevitable heartbreaks and heartaches successfully... and help others to do so as well.

Jesus said to a group of anxiety-ridden and heartbroken disciples, "Let not your hearts be troubled...In My Father's house are many mansions...I go to prepare a place for you!" He would say the same to you in your days of difficulty.

I know, for that's what He spoke to me as I experienced my first wife being taken home to Heaven as a young woman and mother of my three young children, and then again when, several years later, my sixteen-year-old daughter was also taken to Heaven.

Through it all, the hope of Heaven was a healing and soothing medicine for my soul. And it continues to keep my outlook bright and my perspective right. So it is truly my delight to be able to share with you about Heaven.

As you learn about and focus on "things above," it will lift your spirits and lighten the load. I guarantee...you watch, you wait, you'll see!!!

Let not your heart be troubled: ye believe in God, believe also in me. In my Father's house are many mansions: if it were not so, I would have told you. I go to prepare a place for you…that where I am, there ye may be also.

John 14:1-3

Table of Contents

And Israel said unto Joseph, Behold, I die; but God shall be with you, and bring you again unto the land of your fathers.

Chapter One

Behold I Die, But...

There comes a moment in the life of every man when he becomes keenly and acutely aware of his mortality. In the text before us, Jacob is at just such a point. In light of this, please notice with me four elements in his words to his son Joseph...

A Sobering Realization

> And Israel said unto Joseph, Behold, I die....
>
> *Genesis 48:21*

At 147 years of age, it was Jacob's body, no doubt, that let him know the end of his life was near.

I know the feeling. When I was younger, I could eat as much as I wanted. It was wonderful! In college, just about every single night after track practice, we'd all go to Love's Barbecue and order hot fudge sundaes—not just ordinary ones, but the specialty of the house: fifteen-gallon sundaes. And they didn't affect me at all.

Then something happened when I hit middle age. No longer could I eat like that without consequences. I can't explain it—but you can certainly observe it!

Young people don't understand this, but at some point in every man's life, he realizes his days are numbered. And such was the case for Jacob.

Confident Expectation

...But God shall be with you....

Genesis 48:21

"Behold I die," said Jacob, "but God shall be with you."

What a fantastic thing it is for us to be able to say to our children, "Behold I die, but God will see you through. I guarantee it because He has seen me through."

Because Jacob was one who had many failings, tons of shortcomings, and all sorts of problems, he was one who knew that God's faithfulness was not dependent upon his own deservedness. Jacob was a man who knew, even when he was failing and faltering, that God would be faithful, that God would come through. And he passed that assurance on to his son, Joseph.

Due to the aging of the baby boomer generation, you may have noticed that there seems to be a flood of life insurance advertisements lately. Let me tell you, as important as it might be to have life insurance, it's infinitely more important to have life assurance, to be able to say to your son, your daughter, and your grandchildren, "You will make it through because, even as God has been faithful to me, He will be faithful to you."

Don't settle for a piece of the rock from Prudential, gang. Seek the peace of the Rock of Ages. Being in good hands with Allstate doesn't compare to being in the good hands of the Almighty. Dad, listen. Grandpa, take heed. Nothing is more important for your family than your confident expectation that the same God who walks with you every step of the way will do the same for them.

Personal Application

...And bring you again unto the land of your fathers.

Genesis 48:21

Jacob had problems just as we do. Jacob had troubles and inconsistencies just like ours. Nonetheless, he was able to say, "Joseph, God is going to bring you to the land of your fathers."

Mom, Dad—where's your land? It's important that you know because that's where your kids and grandchildren will land when you're gone. If your land is the Kingdom, if you have a love for the Lord, if you're a student of the Word, if you pray and seek first the Kingdom day after day, that's where your kids and grandchildren will land. Conversely, chances are, statistics prove, and experience has shown that if your land is Tinseltown, Rockin' Rodeo, or HBO, those are the places your kids will end up.

Ultimately, the "land of the fathers" is the land of the Father. "In my Father's house are many mansions," Jesus said, "If it were not so, I would have told you. I go to prepare a place for you" (John 14:2). That's where I desperately desire my kids to land. Therefore, being in my forties, I must be vigilant. The stakes are too high to do otherwise—not just for me, but also for my kids and grandchildren.

Oh, I'm Jacob. I still have struggles, failures, and problems. But I'm also Israel—governed by God because I've committed my heart and life to Him. And such is my desire and prayer for those who follow me.

Glorious Continuation

> Moreover I have given to thee one portion above thy brethren, which I took out of the hand of the Amorite with my sword and with my bow.
>
> *Genesis 48:22*

"I'm giving you an extra portion," Jacob says, "a parcel of property I took with my bow and sword from the Amorite." Here's the problem, Bible students: there's no record of Jacob ever doing this. Not only is there no mention in Scripture that Jacob ever took the territory of an Amorite, but doing so was not even in his nature. Esau was the hunter and the warrior, but Jacob was a man who dwelt in tents and cooked. So, what did Jacob mean when he said he took territory with his bow and sword?

The language indicates that this speaks of an event that would take place in the future, an event so certain to happen that Jacob speaks of it as though it had already taken place.

Romans 8 tells us we are glorified. Have we actually physically been glorified? No. But it's going to happen with such certainty that the Bible speaks as though it has already taken place. So too, Jacob is saying, "The portion of land I took with my bow and sword is yours. The foundation has been laid, and what you do will be a continuation of who I am."

Last Sunday, when I was taken violently ill after first service, I called my son, Peter-John, and said, "PJ, you're on." Listening to him on the radio, I was so blessed. Then Sunday night, so many young people opened their hearts to

Jesus and were baptized, and the oldest person in charge of the service was twenty-two-year-old Peter-John.

God is raising up a generation that will take more territory, see farther, do better, claim a bigger portion as they stand on our shoulders and go on to greater victory.

That's why I'm so glad I'm a believer. I know those who come after me—my sons and daughters in my family and in the faith—will do better than I have done. They'll take territory I was unable to claim. They'll do things I could never do.

Our kids, precious people, will do better than us because God takes His people from glory to greater glory. That's His promise. That's His way.

And I can't wait.

A good name is better than precious ointment;
and the day of death than the day of one's
birth.

Ecclesiastes 7:1

Chapter Two

Happy "Deathday" to You

I find myself frequently thanking the Lord for hot, running water. This was something I used to take for granted and for which I rarely thanked the Lord. That was before we moved into a cabin in the Applegate Valley. It was a wonderful place to live; yet, for two summers running, we experienced a drought. Consequently, the spring from which our water came dried up, causing us to bathe in the creek. So from that time on, my appreciation for hot showers has never abated.

When the Book of Ecclesiastes was written, Solomon did not have hot, running water. In fact, there were very few bathtubs at all, which made for a distinct aroma throughout the community. But if you were wealthy enough, with expensive ointments or perfume, you could mask the odor somewhat. These precious ointments did three things...

First, by concealing one's own aroma, they made one socially agreeable.

Secondly, they made one spiritually identifiable. In Exodus 30, we read of a precious ointment called "holy anointing oil." Made of cinnamon, myrrh, and other sweet spices, the priests were the only ones to wear this particular ointment. I find this helpful in understanding what the Lord wants to do in our lives, for the anointing oil, emblematic of the anointing of the Spirit, is a sweet fragrance.

Finally, precious ointments made one recognizable as financially stable. In the days before savings accounts or treasury bonds, when a person had money, he would often invest it in precious ointments. Always in demand, their value remained high. Thus, when Mary of Bethany poured an alabaster container full of perfume over Jesus, she was, in effect, emptying her bank account—which is why Jesus said, "Wherever this gospel shall be preached, this act of love and costly worship will be spoken of" (see Mark 14:9).

Precious ointments. See them in the context of Solomon's day. Yet what does he say in our text? There is something better than precious ointment. That is, a good name. Now, when most of us read this, we equate a good name with a good reputation. But when you study it more carefully, I think you'll discover that's not really the deepest meaning of this verse. You see, a good reputation is not better than costly ointment because a good reputation is that which can be easily taken away.

Ask the patriarchs or the prophets. The people of Israel slandered the vast majority of the prophets mercilessly. Their reputations were dragged through the mud. Accusations and condemnations, innuendoes and attacks abounded. Their reputations were often so marred, the people would rise up against the Old Testament prophets and stone them.

I see Jesus as the epitome of someone who was absolutely good, and yet did He have a good reputation? Philippians 2 says Jesus humbled Himself and made Himself of no reputation. In fact, the community around Him hurled insults at Him, calling Him a glutton, a winebibber, and a demonized individual who did miracles only through the power of Beelzebub.

What then is Solomon saying when he states that a good name is better than precious ointment?

If you have opened your heart and received Jesus as your Lord, don't you know that's more important than popularity, than ministry, than financial stability? If your name is written in the Book of Life, then you have a good name (Revelation 21).

Revelation 2 tells us that those who are in the Book of Life not only have a good name, but they will receive a new name. I'm looking forward to a brand new name, a brand new identity—new papers, new social security cards, new pictures, and a change of image. When we get to Heaven, folks, you won't call me Jon. We'll address each other with the names that the Lord has reserved for us and will reveal to us in that day. Why? Because all the stuff associated with our present name is tarnished, tainted, and weird. I am so looking forward to a fresh start eternally with a new name and a new countenance. It's going to be wonderful to have a new identity!

As the essence of the high priestly ministry, Jesus has our names written on the breastplate over His heart (Exodus 28). Thus, if your name is written in the Book of Life, it is on the Lord's heart as well.

Not only is your name written in the Book of Life, not only is it written over the heart of our High Priest, but it is also engraved in the palm of His hand (Isaiah 49:16). Therefore, no matter where you're at, no matter what this week has held for you, the Lord isn't saying, "Oops, I forgot to watch over you. I forgot all about your situation. I wasn't aware of the crisis you were going through."

No, your name is—

Etched in His hand,

Inscribed on His heart, and

Written in His Book.

When the disciples came back from their first missionary trip, saying, "Lord, You should have seen us. We cast out demons. We raised the dead. We saw miracles happening," Jesus said, "Don't rejoice in any of those things, but rejoice in the fact that your names are written in the Book of Life" (see Luke 10:20).

That's what still matters today. How many miracles you did, how many people you witnessed to, how many mistakes you made, how many sins you committed are not the issue of why you are here today. We're to worship the Lord because, by His grace, our names are written in the Book of Life. Oh, how ministry, popularity, and financial stability pale in comparison to the fact that we're saved and going to Heaven.

Why do I feel this is the correct interpretation of "a good name is better than precious ointment"? I believe the next phrase confirms it: "and the day of death than the day of one's birth."

If your name is written in the Lamb's Book of Life, I want to wish you a happy "deathday" because our text declares the day of death is better than the day of birth. The day of one's birth is wonderful—with one's entire life stretching out before him. But you know what else? As I anticipated the birth of another child in our own family, I realized he or she was going to have some heavy trials and difficulties ahead because life is hard. It just is. There's going to be hurts, disappointments, sin, sorrow, and tragedies. Oh, I rejoiced in the day of my child's birth—but I also knew the journey ahead for him or her would be hard.

As I boarded the plane for the flight from Australia to San

Francisco, I could sense the excitement as everyone found their places and settled down in the seats at the outset of the fifteen-hour journey. But after an hour or two, as we hit some turbulence in the sky, many of us reached for the air bags. Then the person two rows back got nervous and started chain smoking. The movie finally came on, but it was some R-rated film. When the food appeared, it wasn't exactly what we were hoping for. After about the eighth or ninth hour, we began feeling sticky and cramped. As I watched the faces in the cabin, I observed the wear and tear of frayed nerves and thin patience as we all grew weary of the journey.

But when the pilot said, "We'll be landing in San Francisco in five minutes," the spirit of the cabin suddenly picked up. Smiles returned, barf bags were put away. We were home.

Folks, that is why Solomon says better is a "deathday" than a birthday. The queasiness ceases. The smoking stops. The R-rated films are over. We're home.

The "deathday" is not only better than your birthday, but it is better than your best day. Think of the best day of your life.

"The best day of my life was when I turned twenty-one and could do whatever I wanted," you say.

But as wonderful as that day might have seemed to you at that time, wait until you die and see the Lord. When we see Him, we shall be like Him. No more struggling with the flesh. No more saying, "Why did I say that? Why didn't I do that? Why did I fall into that?" In Heaven, we will at last truly come of age.

Perhaps you say, "My best day was the day I got my inheritance." You just wait. Peter says we have an inheritance which is undefiled and incorruptible waiting for us in Heaven (I Peter 1:4). I'm convinced that the majority of us will be shocked when we see the rewards the Lord has waiting for us. Those who think they'll be lucky just to make it in will be amazed to hear the Lord say, "You said this kind word, and you ministered that kind touch. You helped your neighbor, cared for your kids, and hung in there in your marriage. Well done, good and faithful servant. Enter into My joy!"

Perhaps the best day of your life was your wedding day. But at the Marriage of the Lamb, you'll say, "All right! This is what I longed for all along." You see, as with any relationship on earth, marriage holds tremendous happiness—but also real hurts. Not so in Heaven. That is why I am so looking forward to becoming the Bride of Christ. I'm looking forward to someone else paying the bills, figuring out what to do, and answering the questions. It will be oh, so glorious.

Truly, because the day you see Jesus will so far exceed your best day on earth, the day of your death will be the best day of your life.

And they that be wise shall shine as the brightness of the firmament; and they that turn many to righteousness as the stars for ever and ever.

Daniel 12:3

Chapter Three

Sharing and Shining

As we come to the close of yet another year, the media will begin to give us its evaluations and expectations for famous people. *TIME* magazine will name its Man of the Year. *Sports Illustrated* will name its Sportsman of the Year. And the hosts of *the Academy Awards®* will announce the winners of the much-coveted *Oscars*.

But, because I would venture to guess that few, if any, of us could name last year's Man of the Year or the MVP of last year's Super Bowl, I think most of us are realizing that the superstars of the world soon become shooting stars. That is, they burst upon the pages of magazines and the screens of TVs, but soon burn out and are forgotten.

In Daniel 12:3, however, we read of stars which will not burn out but which will shine forever.

> And they that be wise shall shine as the brightness of the firmament; and they that turn many to righteousness as the stars for ever and ever.

These true stars, which will shine forever and ever, are not Oscar winners, but soul-winners.

In I Corinthians, Paul picks up the same analogy and shines more light on this subject when he writes,

> There is one glory of the sun, and another
> glory of the moon, and another glory of the
> stars: for one star differeth from another star
> in glory. So also is the resurrection of the
> dead. It is sown in corruption; it is raised in
> incorruption: it is sown in dishonour; it is
> raised in glory: it is sown in weakness; it is
> raised in power.
>
> *I Corinthians 15:41-43*

The word "glory" means "outshining." In other words, Paul tells us there will be differing degrees of brightness, different degrees of intensity concerning these stars which will shine forever.

Indeed, everyone in Heaven will be totally, completely happy, thrilled, and elated beyond words. Every tear shall be wiped from every eye. A smile will be upon every face. Heaven will be glorious, wonderful, and perfect.

When my son Benjamin was twelve-months old, he got the biggest kick out of hitting pots and pans with a wooden spoon. Out of curiosity, I took the same spoon, the same pots and pans, and hit them for all I was worth. Yet, although this tickled Benny, it didn't do a whole lot for me. Why? Because I wasn't twelve-months old anymore. Therefore, my capacity to understand and enjoy life was far beyond beating pots and pans. My world is bigger, my experience is greater.

So too, in Heaven we're all going to be happy. But our capacities for happiness will differ. We'll all be filled to the brim with joy, but the size of our containers will vary. Some will be great big barrels; others will be little thimbles. Both will be filled, but the capacities will be different. Some will be in Heaven with a limited potential to enjoy and experience eternity. Oh, they were saved on earth, but they did nothing with their faith. They rendered no real service to the Kingdom. They just sort of cruised through life. They'll make it to Heaven, but they'll be like Benny—banging away on pots and pans. Others, because they were wise, because they served the Lord radically, will shine like stars—huge in their ability to enjoy eternity.

Here's the question: If we know turning people to righteousness is wise and that we'll shine as the stars forever as a result, why don't we do it? We've been trained. We've taken classes and seminars. We know the theories. We even know the Scriptures. But when it comes down to getting the job done, we so often don't. Why?

I'm convinced it's for one simple reason. We have been mistaken concerning what winning souls is all about. We have looked at witnessing as confrontation: telling people they're sinners headed for Hell unless they get saved—only to see them put up walls and walk away.

There's a better way. Consider Numbers 10, where we see an illustration of witnessing, not as confrontation, but as invitation...

> And Moses said unto Hobab, the son of Raguel the Midianite, Moses' father in law, We are journeying unto the place of which the LORD said, I will give it you: come thou with us, and we will do thee good: for the LORD hath spoken good concerning Israel.
>
> *Numbers 10:29*

Headed for the Promised Land, Moses didn't say to his brother-in-law, "You better turn from your ways, you sinful

Midianite, you pagan idolater." No, he said, "We're going to a good place. Come with us."

So too, we can say to our co-workers and neighbors, our family and friends, "We're going to a good land. We're going to Heaven. Come with us."

Truly, Heaven is going to be absolutely incredible. It gives me great hope to realize that this earth is as bad as we'll ever have it. We're only passing through this wilderness, headed for a better land indeed.

Astronomers now have conclusive proof that there are entire galaxies beyond ours which are made of compressed carbon—or diamonds. How amazing it will be to explore the outer parts of the universe with new bodies custom-made for such excursions. No wonder Paul said eyes have not seen nor ears heard the things God has prepared for those who love Him (I Corinthians 2:9).

"Come with us," Moses said to Hobab. But what did Hobab say?

> And he said unto him, I will not go; but I will depart to mine own land, and to my kindred.
>
> *Numbers 10:30*

Does this sound familiar to any of you who have tried to witness?

Moses could have said to Hobab, "Fine. Stay in Midian. Get wiped out." But I love Moses here, for after extending an invitation, he gives an exhortation...

> And he said, Leave us not, I pray thee; forasmuch as thou knowest how we are to

encamp in the wilderness, and thou mayest
be to us instead of eyes. And it shall be, if
thou go with us, yea, it shall be, that what
goodness the LORD shall do unto us, the
same will we do unto thee.

Numbers 10:31-32

"Don't leave us," said Moses. "Don't go back to your
people. You know the dangers and pitfalls of the land
through which we're traveling. You can be eyes for us."

Is this a lack of faith on the part of Moses? After all,
hadn't the Lord promised to be with them, to lead them, to
provide for them?

I do not believe Moses is in any way showing a lack
of faith. Rather, he is changing his tactics in witnessing.
Instead of saying, "You should come with us," he's saying,
"Please come with us. We value you. We see your potential.
We can use you."

Jesus did the same thing when He asked the woman
whom He would draw to a saving knowledge of Himself if
she would draw Him some water (John 4). In so doing, I
believe He was saying, "I value what you can give to Me even
as I am about to give something invaluable to you."

So too, no matter the arena, we can say to the people
with whom we come into contact, "Come with us. We need
you." To the doctor, we can say, "We need doctors like you
on our missionary teams." To the businessman, we can say,
"We could use your financial expertise to help people who
are drowning in debt." To the preschool teacher, we can say,
"Come with us. We have little ones who need your care."

Too often, all people hear from Christians is, "You're
a sinner bound for Hell. It's too bad that don't have it

together like we do"—and we wonder why they won't join us. For some reason, we have been taught witnessing is confrontation. It's not. It's invitation.

We get to share the Gospel. We get to share the Good News with parents and kids, with neighbors and friends. We get to say, "I know there are things you have done in your past which haunt you. But I have good news for you: you're forgiven. Because of what Jesus did on the Cross, every single sin you've ever committed is forgiven by God" (see I John 2:2).

The greatest secret I know in winning souls is this: treat people as if they're already saved. Tell them what you're learning. Open up to them. Share with them. Sinners loved to be around Jesus because He would talk to them about the Kingdom and eternity as if they were headed there. Rather than point His finger at them, He shared with them. And as a result, they followed Him.

> Now Heber the Kenite, which was of the children of Hobab the father in law of Moses, had severed himself from the Kenites, and pitched his tent unto the plain of Zaanaim, which is by Kedesh.
>
> *Judges 4:11*

Evidently, Hobab changed his mind—for here are his descendants in the Promised Land. So too, when we start inviting and encouraging people rather than confronting them, like Hobab, they change their minds.

Be like Jesus. Be like Moses. The walls will come down. The ice will melt. You'll see souls won. And you'll shine throughout eternity as a star with great glory.

Let not your heart be troubled: ye believe in God, believe also in me. In my Father's house are many mansions: if it were not so, I would have told you. I go to prepare a place for you. And if I go and prepare a place for you, I will come again, and receive you unto myself; that where I am, there ye may be also.

John 14:1-3

Chapter Four

Heaven

No doubt the disciples were deeply distressed, for there in the Upper Room Jesus began to inform them of some troubling news:

That one would betray Him;

That Peter would deny Him; and

That He would leave them.

Yet, as the room fills with confusion, Jesus looks at His disciples and says, "Let not your heart be troubled. Heaven is the key."

According to an April 24, 2000, *Washington Post* article, eighty-eight percent of all Americans believe in a literal place called Heaven—an important statistic because imagine what our society would be like if we didn't believe in Heaven...

A society that didn't believe in Heaven would be obsessed with youth. It would spend hundreds of thousands of dollars trying to look, stay, and feel young through plastic surgery, diets, and exercise programs.

A society that didn't believe in Heaven would spend billions of dollars on life support systems to delay facing an unknown future.

In a society that didn't believe in Heaven, crime would soar without fear of eternal judgment.

The theology of a society which didn't believe in Heaven would be based upon the here and now—on health and prosperity.

Wait a minute. We are that culture, because although our generation gives lip service to the idea of Heaven, we do not live out the reality of Heaven.

Why isn't Heaven a reality? I suggest the following reasons...

Ministry

There is tremendous pressure in the ministry presently to "teach to the times," to "scratch where it itches." "No one wants to hear about Heaven," we are told. "Preach to people here and now."

Accused of being old-fashioned because he always preached on Heaven, a classic English preacher gave this response: "While everyone is preaching to the times, may not this poor soul speak for eternity?"[1]

Such is my feeling. Let others talk about cultural relevancy—I desire to be a voice for eternity. The Bible speaks of Heaven 557 times; it's a fundamental, foundational truth.

Society

Ours is the first generation to teach that, materially, one can have Heaven on earth...

"Your life will be perfect if you use Arrid Extra Dry," we are told. Or "If you drive a convertible, girls will flock around you."

Although we fall for this pitch time and time again, each time, we rediscover that nothing on this earth is substantial; nothing this side of eternity can do more than whet our appetite for Heaven.

Has your soul ever been stirred simply by watching the water cascade down a waterfall? Has your heart ever been overwhelmed by the beauty of the sun setting into the ocean? Have you ever been moved to tears by the "Hallelujah Chorus"?

I suggest these are feelings common to man. And I suggest that what they rekindle is a vague, foggy, misty memory of a place called Eden—

Where there was no sin, no sorrow, no disease, and no death;

> Where man walked with God in the cool of the day;

> Where things were right.

When such a memory stirs within me, I feel like a frog which has been cursed. I'm waiting for the prince to come and kiss me before I croak. And that's where our society is. We know there has to be something more because our experiences with true beauty and with true reality are always so fleeting.

"What happened to the waterfall experience?" we cry.

> "What happened to the sunset?

> What happened to the "Hallelujah Chorus"?

> Why do they elude me?

> Where's my prince?"

Good news! Jesus Christ, the Prince of Peace, is a frog-kisser. How do I know? Because in the moment of confusion, He says to us, as He said to His disciples, "Don't lose sight of the big picture. The solution to your confusion lies in a single word: Heaven."

As always, Jesus was right, for whenever we consider the ramifications of Heaven, our confusion turns to clarity, our despair to delight, and our fear to faith...

The Perspective of Eternity

Believers are sometimes accused of being so heavenly-minded that they're no earthly good.

The Bible, however, teaches just the opposite—that we won't be any earthly good until we are heavenly-minded because, as Paul points out, "if in this life only we have hope in Christ, we are of all men most miserable" (I Corinthians 15:19).

This one who was shipwrecked, beaten, imprisoned, starved, stoned, and left for dead declared, "If there is no Heaven, then life is miserable."

Perhaps it was his proximity to death on so many occasions which prompted him to write, "Set your affections on things above" (Colossians 3:2)—for once Paul experienced even a taste of Heaven, nothing else mattered to him except to run the race, to win the prize, and to live with eternity in view.

The Puzzle of Prosperity

Suppose you're waiting to board a flight to Portland and the pilot walks in, saying, "You are going to have the flight of your life. Smooth sailing all the way! I guarantee, we won't hit one pocket of turbulence. You will have quadraphonic earphones, an Epicurean experience with a seven-course meal, and your choice of first-run movies. There's only one problem: we haven't figured out how to land. We've tried it a thousand times, and everybody dies—but while you're in the air, I promise your flight will be smooth and your experience fulfilling."

At this point, a second pilot enters the boarding area, saying, "I can't promise smooth sailing. In fact, from here to Portland, you'll no doubt hit some bumps and you might even have the urge to 're-gurge.' However, we have a perfect landing record, and we will get you to your destination safely. Guaranteed."

Which plane would you board?

To some, the question itself poses a problem, for like David, they feel envious of the foolish when they see the prosperity of the wicked (Psalm 73:3). What's the answer? It is found in the sanctuary of God—for it is there that David understood that although the wicked were experiencing smooth sailing presently, they were headed for Hell eternally (Psalm 73:17-19).

The 1991 Oakland/Berkeley Hills fire consumed million-dollar homes, leaving nothing. "I not only lost my house, I lost everything," an elderly man was quoted as saying. "My life's savings were in cash which I kept in my home. My wife and I were very careful all of our years to save our money. We were saving for a rainy day, never counting on a fiery night."

Listen, gang, for the unbeliever, life on earth is as good as it gets. But for the believer, life on earth is the worst it gets.

The Promise of Productivity

Most people have the idea that Heaven is sort of like a long, Sunday afternoon nap—plucking a few strings on a harp, eating a grape or two now and then, lounging around on a white cloud. Not true, for in Heaven you will be able to experience to the fullest extent the desires of your heart.

Maybe you just love music, but you don't really have the gift to do a lot with it. When you get to Heaven, watch out! You can own a choir! You can sing gloriously to your heart's content. Maybe your thing is gardening. In Heaven, the grass really is greener. No weeds! Or maybe you're a people person. The people you know here, you'll know there.

How do I know this? Because we're not going to be dumber in Heaven than we are here. Won't our bodies be changed? Yes, but look at Jesus—when He came back from the dead, although He walked through a wall, Thomas still recognized Him immediately (John 20:28).

As for those in Heaven we haven't yet met, nametags will be unnecessary, as it seems we will instinctively know people there. Why do I think this? Because on the Mount of Transfiguration, Jesus didn't say, "Peter, James, and John, I'd like you to meet Moses and Elijah. Moses and Elijah, say 'Hi' to Peter, James, and John." There were no formal introductions, yet Peter, James, and John knew intuitively that it was Moses and Elijah talking to Jesus (Matthew 17:4).

Productivity like we've never known awaits us in Heaven, where we will rule angels, govern cities, and manage the universe (Revelation 22:5).

The Reality of Relativity

The source of the greatest frustration of people presently is the lack of time—which is why we constantly find ourselves saying, "Where did the time go?" or "My kids are growing up too fast," or "There's so much I want to do, but I can't find the time."

Do the birds complain about the air in which they fly? Do the fish complain about the sea? Only man complains about his environment because it is one in which he doesn't belong. Time frustrates him because he is made for a timeless eternity. C.S. Lewis said it best when he wrote, "If I find in myself a desire which no experience in this world can satisfy, the most probable explanation is that I was made for another world."[2]

The fact that, according to Ecclesiastes, there is neither past, present, nor future in eternity means Heaven is a continual "now." How can this be? Ask Albert Einstein. His Theory of Relativity has more to do with eternity than he probably could have guessed, for in propounding that when one travels at the speed of light, time stops, he validated the fact that because God is Himself light (I John 1:5), in His presence, time ceases.

Thus, if time—man's biggest frustration on earth—is non-existent in Heaven, we can be sure every lesser frustration will be obliterated as well. Heaven will truly be absolutely, wonderfully, and incredibly perfect.

"How can it be perfect if those I love are still on earth?" some ask.

If you put a glob of peanut butter at one end of a shoebox, ants at the other end, and a maze in between, you would see the ants begin to wind their way through the maze, journeying toward their celestial peanut butter glob city. You would see it all: the beginning, the journey, and the end. But they wouldn't. All they would see is the next wall in front of them.

So too, those in Heaven see the whole thing unfolding simultaneously. Not only are events occurring concurrently, but from their perspective, we are already standing beside them in eternity.

Still others are concerned about the people who won't be in Heaven. "How can it be Heaven if I know people I care about aren't there?" they wonder.

Concerning the Amalekites who were hassling the people of Israel, the Lord said, "I will destroy them and remove their memory from your minds" (see Deuteronomy 25:19).

The Psalmist picks up the same theme when, in six occasions, he talks specifically about the "blotting out of the names of those who are against God." Thus, on the model of the Amalekites and the sentiment of the Psalmist, I suggest you will not even remember the people who are not saved.

The Answer to Inequity

Heaven is the place where we will at last have all our questions answered. Why was this person born severely retarded? Why was that person born to starvation? Why wasn't this person healed when we prayed in faith? Why was that baby allowed to be conceived, only to be aborted? Why, why, why?

Psalm 139 tells us that all of our days are written in a book. Could it be that the "book" is what science now calls the DNA genetic code—the strand wherein is packed all of one's characteristics, appearance, and entire being? So much information is crammed into the DNA genetic code that it would fill at least a million typed pages, according to the Nobel Foundation. Consequently, could it be that even if a baby is aborted or born prematurely, his or her genetic code will be fully revealed and realized in Heaven?

"Hang on," Jesus said. "It's not over yet.

The first will be last;

The last will be first; and

The score will be settled."

The Response to Opportunity

Maybe you've had opportunity to hear Jesus say, "I am the Way, the Truth, and the Life,"—but you don't care. God will give you your way if you're not interested. You'll be allowed to go where you want—but know this: Hell is not a party. It's a place of eternal weeping, wailing, and gnashing of teeth (Matthew 8:12).

But for you who have taken Jesus up on His offer as the Way, the Truth, and the Life, congratulations! You're going to Heaven! So, let not your heart be troubled.

Get ready.

Get packed.

Get set.

We're going home!

And it came to pass, as we went to prayer, a certain damsel possessed with a spirit of divination met us, which brought her masters much gain by soothsaying: the same followed Paul and us, and cried, saying, These men are the servants of the most high God, which shew unto us the way of salvation. And this did she many days. But Paul, being grieved, turned and said to the spirit, I command thee in the name of Jesus Christ to come out of her. And he came out the same hour.

Acts 16:16-18

Chapter Five

Heavenly Vision

When the 1992 election ended, political pundits weighed in with their theories on why President Bush didn't win the election. Essentially, they are offering two reasons: one is the lingering recession, but secondly—and perhaps more importantly—they cite the president's failure to articulate vision. In fact, you might remember that President Bush himself told reporters upon taking office in 1989 that he had trouble with the vision thing.

In Proverbs 29:18, we are told that without vision, people perish. Literally, "people run wild," or as seen in some marginal notes, "people run naked." Thus, vision is necessary for every president, and for every person—for without it, people run wildly, aimlessly, and shamefully.

"Write the vision, Habakkuk," said the Lord, "and make it plain so he that runneth by may be able to read it" (see Habakkuk 2:2). In other words, "Write the vision so clearly that even the person who runs rapidly might be able to understand it"—for without vision, people wander in mediocrity and meander in mundanity.

Nowhere is necessity of vision seen more clearly than in the life of the Apostle Paul. He had purpose and meaning because he understood from the moment of his conversion the heavenly vision for his life.

Perhaps you're saying, "Good for Paul. I'm glad he had a vision from Heaven. But I have never seen the Lord physically as Paul did, or heard His voice audibly as Paul did. So how am I supposed to get vision like Paul did? If vision is necessary for a productive, successful life, how am I supposed to receive vision personally?"

I have good news for you today: Paul the apostle, the one who had heavenly vision, was also the one who said, "Follow me as I follow Christ" (see I Corinthians 11:1). In other words, the vision the Lord gave Paul, recorded in our text, is the vision the Lord intends for you and me as well. Paul's vision is to be our vision.

Paul's Calling

> But rise, and stand upon thy feet: for I have appeared unto thee for this purpose, to make thee a minister and a witness....
>
> *Acts 26:16*

After the Lord appeared to Paul on the road to Damascus, He said, "Here's what you are to be, Paul: a minister and a witness." The Greek word for minister means "under-rower." It's a word which described the guys in the galley of a large ship who, although they were unseen, unnoticed, and un-applauded, rowed steadily and moved the ship to its ultimate destination.

And Paul's commission is for you as well. You see, Jesus said, "You have not chosen Me, but I have chosen you and ordained you, that you should bring forth much fruit" (see John 15:16). Whoever you are—man, woman, teenager, young person—if you are a believer in Christ, He has ordained you into ministry.

We are not only to be ministers, but secondly, we are to be witnesses. A witness is one who goes into the courtroom and simply shares what he or she has seen. The Lord did not call you to be an attorney, arguing the case, or a judge, handing down a verdict. The Lord simply called you to be a witness—to tell people what He has done for you personally.

When I don't live up to that calling, my life becomes dull, incredibly ordinary, and meaningless. But when I minister and witness, a funny thing happens: I get back more than I give. Not surprising, since Jesus said, "the measure that you give out shall be meted back to you" (see Luke 6:38).

Paul's Mission

> To open their eyes, and to turn them from darkness to light, and from the power of Satan unto God....
>
> *Acts 26:18*

To Open Men's Eyes

Why do people need their eyes opened? Because they have been blinded by sin.

As Samson laid his head on Delilah's lap, he sinned by sharing with her the secret of his strength. "If you cut my hair," he said, "I'll be like any man." You know the story. Delilah reached for the scissors and began snipping. When Samson awoke, Scripture says, "he knew not that the Spirit had departed from him" (see Judges 16:20). He thought he could take the Philistines on, but instead, they took him down. They placed him in fetters, poked out his eyes, and led him to the granary where, hitched to a grinding stone like a common ox, he went round and round in circles.

That's what sin does: it binds, it blinds, and it makes life a grind. "What's my life about? Why am I here? Why should I get out of bed?" we say as we go round and round.

Sin blinds people. First, it blinds people to their need for Jesus...

"Do you enjoy being a preacher?" asked the cashier.

"Yes," I answered. "As a matter of fact, I love what I do."

"Well, I was raped two years ago," she said as she started to cry, "and people have tried to get me to church, but church is a crutch."

"You're right," I said. "But it's more than a crutch. Church is an ambulance, an emergency room, a hospital, and a surgical team." It's for people who realize they're hurt—either by their own sin or the sin of others. It's for people who say,

"We need a Helper.

We need a Healer.

We need a Savior."

I don't know what she's going to do, but I'm so thankful I was able to share with her the reality that Jesus is the answer.

Secondly, sin blinds people to the nature of Jesus. It's amazing the misconceptions people have about our Lord. They think He is some kind of cosmic killjoy who looks down from Heaven, worried that someone, somewhere, might be having fun.

Nothing could be further from the truth. Jesus said, "I have come that you might have life and life abundantly." "You shall know the truth, and the truth shall set you free" (see John 10:10, 8:32). Jesus came to set people free—not to put a religious trip on them.

How? To be free, to get a fresh start, "you must be born again" (John 3:7, NKJV).

A lady called her husband and said, "Honey, the car isn't working."

"What's wrong?" he asked.

"There's water in the carburetor," she said.

"Water in the carburetor? That's impossible. The cooling system doesn't touch the carburetor. There can't be water in the carburetor."

"Yes," insisted his wife. "There's definitely water in the carburetor."

"Well, I'll come home and take a look," he said. "Where's the car?"

"At the bottom of the pool," she answered.

You might disagree with the divine diagnosis, but the Bible says that although you have been buried in the pool of iniquity and the sea of sin, it is the desire of the Lord's heart to rescue you, to breathe life into you, and to put you on your feet once again.

That's the nature of Jesus.

> To open their eyes, and to turn them from darkness to light, and from the power of Satan unto God....
>
> *Acts 26:18*

To Turn Men's Lives

Not only was Paul to open men's eyes, he was to turn men's lives from darkness to light, from the power of Satan to the power of God. You see, two kingdoms dwell simultaneously on this earth: the kingdom of Light and Love, which is the kingdom of God, and the kingdom of darkness and death, which is the kingdom of Satan. Every man is in one of these two kingdoms. No one is neutral, for Jesus said, "He that is not with me is against me...." (Matthew 12:30). Therefore, if you are not in the kingdom of God—if He is not your Lord and King and Leader—then you are in Satan's kingdom of death and darkness.

<u>Satan loves darkness—</u>

<u>Most crimes are committed at night.</u>

The period in history when people didn't worship God is called the Dark Ages.

A continent which has not been exposed to the Gospel is called a dark continent.

Hell is called outer darkness (Matthew 8:12).

Some people think Hell is a bunch of guys playing poker and telling dirty jokes. Nothing could be further from the truth. Astrologists tell us about the existence of black holes so dense that nothing escapes their gravitational pull—not even light itself.

When the guide turns out the lights in the Oregon Caves, there's an absolute absence of light. So dark, you can't see your hand in front of your face, it's a darkness which seems to have a substance of its own—you can feel it.

Hell is like that. In Hell, no one will see a thing—for a day, a month, a year, a century, a millennium, a billion millenniums. Men who choose to live in darkness on earth will spend eternity surrounded by darkness in Hell. That's why Paul said, "My ministry, my job, my vision is to open men's eyes and to turn men's lives from darkness to light, from the power of Satan to the power of God."

"Wait," you say. "I may not be a follower of God—but neither am I dominated by Satan. I'm master of my own destiny, captain of my own fate." The Bible says otherwise. According to the Word, people who aren't walking with the Lord are actually opposing or hurting themselves through their lifestyles and attitudes, their activities and habits (II Timothy 2:25).

In an issue of *USA Today* was a picture of the former Mr. Universe with his arm around the former Mr. America. These two men were traveling across the country as a newly married couple, sharing the validity of alternative lifestyles. Now, all the while Mr. Universe and Mr. America thought they were controlling their own destinies as self-made men, Satan was letting them win titles and do their thing, knowing that at the right time, he would reel them in.

The Bible says those who think they are self-made are actually captives of him who is able to reel them in at will. How, then, are men freed from Satan's grasp? "You shall know the truth, and the *truth* shall make you free," said Jesus (John 8:32, NKJV, emphasis mine).

"What is truth?" Pontius Pilate asked (John 18:38).

"I am," said Jesus (John 14:6).

Gang, we have the privilege of opening men's eyes to their need for Jesus and to the nature of Jesus. We get to turn men's lives from the power of darkness and the devil to the power of light and the Lord.

How?

Through a principle of physics called the expulsive power of the greater force, which says: if you want to rid a room of darkness, you don't fight against the darkness by trying to karate chop it, rebuke it, or yell at it. You turn on the light, and light—the greater power—will flood the room, expelling the darkness. Jesus said, "I am the light of the world" (John 8:12). Therefore, when a man or a woman opens up his or her heart to Jesus Christ, the light of the Lord naturally drives out the darkness of Satan.

Men's eyes are opened and their lives are turned by the power of the Spirit—not programs, not principles, not procedures. It is the power of the resurrected Lord that works change in a person. It's God's one-step program: get saved, let the Spirit direct your life, and you will be absolutely free.

Men's eyes are opened and their lives are turned by the prayers of the saints. You can witness to people until you're blue in the face, but if their eyes are blinded, they won't receive what you say. How is the blindfold removed? Ephesians 6 says the weapons of our warfare are not fleshly, but spiritual. Prayer is the number one weapon in our arsenal. We can do more than pray, but we can't do anything until we pray.

Men's eyes are opened and their lives are turned by proclaiming the Scriptures. If someone is complaining, tell them the Bible says to give thanks in everything (I Thessalonians 5:18), and watch his reaction. If someone is upset because his candidate didn't win, say, "The Bible says all things work together for good to them that love God" (Romans 8:28), and check out his response. Jesus said, "The words which I speak are spirit and life" (see John 6:63). Share the Word—it's powerful!

A seminary student asked Charles Spurgeon how to defend Scripture against unbelievers, skeptics, and cynics. The three hundred pound preacher laughed aloud and said, "How do you defend the Scriptures? Son, that's like asking how to defend a lion. Just let it out of its cage. It'll defend itself."[3]

How long has it been since you "let the Word out" and shared the Scriptures with an unbeliever? Share the Word—that's where the power is.

Paul's vision was to turn men's eyes and turn men's lives in order that men would experience the forgiveness of sins and the inheritance of faith (Acts 26:18).

Some years back, I read of a broken-hearted father who took out a full-page ad in a Madrid newspaper. It read: "Dear Paco, meet me in front of this newspaper office at noon on Saturday. All is forgiven. I love you. Your father."

The next day scores of young men named Paco were there, each hoping it was his father who said, "I love you. All is forgiven. Come home."

Forgiveness of sin is man's greatest need and God's greatest deed. If you've been saved for a while, this concept might have become dulled in your understanding because you live in the realm of forgiveness; but the world doesn't. "Follow me as I follow Christ," Paul says to you today. Be a minister. Be a sharer.

Open men's eyes and turn men's lives,

In the power of the Spirit,

By the praying of the saints,

Through the proclaiming of the Scriptures.

They will experience forgiveness like they've never known—and you will be fulfilled presently and rewarded eternally.

Every man's work shall be made manifest: for the day shall declare it, because it shall be revealed by fire; and the fire shall try every man's work of what sort it is.

I Corinthians 3:13

Chapter Six

Go for the Gold!

"I'm in big trouble," he said, showing me his wrist grotesquely scarred from the slash he had inflicted upon himself in a recent attempt to take his life.

"Good news," I told him. "Whether you believe in Him or not, God believes in you. He'll change your life completely, totally, and radically if you allow Him. And then He'll use that scar to powerfully speak to others about where you've been and where His grace has brought you."

After he told me a bit of his story—how he had been part of a drug-running group and how his wife had left him because she feared for her life—I took him through the simple verses about salvation from the Book of Romans. He prayed to receive Christ right then.

Truly there was joy in his heart and in his eyes as he realized he was truly set free. And there was certainly joy in Heaven over his repentance (Luke 15:7).

But I would be surprised indeed if there was any joy greater than my own.

Hearts of Joy

"Woe is me if I preach not the Gospel," Paul declared (see I Corinthians 9:16). The idea of woe includes discouragement, depression, and defeat. I will experience all of those emotions if I'm not sharing the Gospel.

I've learned over the years that if I'm not sharing the Gospel, if I'm focusing solely on the Body, on preparing sermons, or on tending the needs of the Fellowship to the exclusion of sharing my faith personally, I descend into a woeful state where things become depressing, heavy, and discouraging. But when I share the good news of the Gospel with someone who doesn't know the Lord, joy fills my soul as I catch a "sneak preview of coming attractions" in Heaven.

I'm convinced that one of the reasons for the holy laughter movement was the Christians craving for a fresh infusion of joy. But they were deceived. Joy doesn't come from Christians getting together and laughing, it comes from seeing people saved. It comes from seeing people rescued from the grip of the enemy. It comes from seeing someone once headed for Hell, now headed for Heaven.

When I am able to lead someone to the Lord, a deep work takes place in my heart very definitely—I am thrilled and filled with indescribable joy.

Crowns of Rejoicing

Not only will there be joy in your heart when God uses you to bring someone to Him, but there will be a crown of gold awaiting you in Heaven (I Thessalonians 2:19).

"So what?" you might be thinking. "I'm not into crowns. I don't even like hats that much."

But I guarantee you won't be saying that in Heaven. I know this because it was after Paul was caught up into the third heaven that he said,

Know ye not that they which run in a race

run all, but one receiveth the prize? So run, that ye may obtain. And every man that striveth for the mastery is temperate in all things. Now they do it to obtain a corruptible crown; but we an incorruptible. I therefore so run, not as uncertainly; so fight I, not as one that beateth the air: but I keep under my body, and bring it into subjection: lest that by any means, when I have preached to others, I myself should be a castaway.

I Corinthians 9:24-27

As one who had been to Heaven and had seen what transpired there, Paul said, "Other people can strive for earthly rewards, but not me. I'm living for Heaven. I'm giving it all I have because I know what's going to happen there."

The crowns we will be given in Heaven are not meant to make a fashion statement, but they will determine what we do throughout eternity. In Luke 19, we see Jesus giving a parable about a man who gave each of his servants a pound. One servant invested his pound and turned it into ten. Another invested his and turned it into five. The third servant, however, buried his pound in the earth. Jesus went on to say that when the master comes back, he will take the pound which the servant buried and give it to the servant who had ten.

"So it is in the Kingdom," He said. "Some will be rulers over ten cities, others over five cities, and others will lose what they had."

"I don't want to rule cities," you might be thinking. Listen, whatever it is to which this refers, it's going to be so grand and glorious that the faithful will say, "Wow! I get to do this? I get to live here? I get to be involved in that just because I was focused on eternity and wasn't living for my reputation or my possessions?"

I promise you, not one of us will say in that day, "Well, this is nice, but I really wish I would have bought a bigger house on earth. I wish I would have done more with my tennis game. I wish I would have spent a little more time playing golf." No! None of us will say that! Instead, we're going to say, "Oh, if only I had known, if only I had been able to understand, if only I had listened, I would have put more of my treasures in Heaven."

If we're wise, we'll seek first the Kingdom, knowing that everything else will take care of itself (Matthew 6:33). If we're wise, we'll put our treasure in Heaven, knowing that our heart will follow (Matthew 6:21). If we're wise, we'll go for the gold of Heaven.

Not only will what I do in the next years affect what I do forever, but it also affects who I'll be. You see, just as there are bright stars, dim stars, and shooting stars in the heavens presently, Paul tells us there will be different stars in Heaven eternally (I Corinthians 15:41-43). That is, although all believers will indeed be in Heaven, although all believers will be completely, absolutely, and totally happy, we will have different capacities for happiness. Some will be filled with joy—to the degree that a thimble can be filled. Others will be filled with joy—to the degree that a barrel can be filled. Like stars, some will shine brightly, while others will shine faintly.

The one who understands that life is short—that what he's craving is found only in Heaven—is the one who puts away his earthly toys and goes for the gold of Heaven in order that he might shine brightly, that he might have a huge capacity to enjoy all of eternity.

Having said this, however, here's what has discouraged

me in years past. The crowns of which Paul speaks seem virtually unattainable, because in our text, we read that all of our works will be tried by fire. The gold, silver, and precious stones which remain will become the crown that determines what I do and who I am, while the wood, hay, and stubble—that which was done with fleshly attitudes and wrong motives—will simply burn up. Now, because everything I do is tainted by my flesh in one way or four others, to one degree or six others, I knew I'd be a faint star in Heaven with a thimble full of joy. Therefore, why shouldn't I simply enjoy this life and live for the things of the world? After all, crowns are truly out of my spiritual ability or reach, aren't they?

The answer, as well as an entirely new perspective, came to me recently when I realized that, because the Lord's throne is a throne of grace (Hebrews 4:16), His reward stand—the Bema Seat—will be characterized by grace as well. And grace makes anything possible...

In Hebrews 11—the listing of God's "Hall of Faith"—I am as amazed by those who are included (e.g., Samson, Jacob, and Barak) as I am by those who are missing (e.g., Elijah, Elisha, Jeremiah, and Deborah). Of those included, consider Rahab. Yes, she hid the spies of Israel, but she also was a liar (Joshua 2:4-5). Therefore, in my opinion, her sin of lying would negate the good she did in hiding the spies. But such is not God's opinion. And the implication of this is huge, for it tells me that it's not a matter of the work we do on earth being either wood, hay, and stubble *or* gold, silver, and precious stones. Rather, it's that in the gold, silver, and precious stones, there will be some wood, hay, and stubble which will be burned away. Truly, when the Lord looks on our works, His eyes of love will suddenly melt the mixed motives with which we did them.

"Look at how beautiful this is!" He'll say.

"What?!" we'll say. "You found gold, silver, and precious stones in that, Lord? I didn't want to preach. I didn't want to share. I did it only because I was expected to. I did it because my wife made me."

"Perhaps," He'll say. "But all I see is gold, silver, and precious stones. You might see lying. But all I see are hidden spies."

Gang, whenever you do anything good, Satan is going to be there whispering in your ear, "Who do you think you're fooling? Your motives aren't right. You're only doing this to receive the applause of men."

But Jesus would say to you, "I am not unrighteous to forget your labor of love" (see Hebrews 6:10). In fact, He said, "If you even give a cold cup of water to a little kid, I'll remember and reward you for that" (see Matthew 10:42).

If we really understood that it is the enemy—a deceiver and a liar—who tells you and me, "Don't go for the gold. It's too hard. You'll never make it," we would continue doing whatever we could do for the Kingdom, knowing the Lord will sort through it to find the gold, silver, and precious stones in whatever we do.

It's not that God winks at sin. It's that He's dealt with it decisively—

By the blood He shed,

By the price He paid, and

By the work He did on Calvary.

Therefore, I can say, "Lord, if even Your reward stand is based on grace, I'm going to do everything I can, all day, every day—be it giving cold water to kids on the street, saying 'God bless you in the mall,' passing out a tract or two, praying with my neighbor, or smiling at the gas station attendant—knowing that You'll be faithful to find any good therein."

Let's go for it, saints. If we do, we'll be amazed by the crowns we receive—crowns we can cast at His feet, crowns which determine our capacity in the Kingdom.

God would have you be free today. He'll sort through everything and anything you do and find gold, silver, and precious stones within. Therefore, don't let the devil talk you out of your eternal perspective. Don't lose sight of the big picture. Enjoy what you're doing for the Lord.

And go for the gold!

For this we say unto you by the word of the Lord, that we which are alive and remain unto the coming of the Lord shall not prevent them which are asleep. For the Lord himself shall descend from heaven with a shout, with the voice of the archangel, and with the trump of God: and the dead in Christ shall rise first: then we which are alive and remain shall be caught up together with them in the clouds, to meet the Lord in the air: and so shall we ever be with the Lord.

I Thessalonians 4:15-17

Chapter Seven

Reasons for the Rapture

On July 20, 1969, astronaut Neil Armstrong left the Apollo Lunar Command Module of Apollo 11 and became the first human to set foot on the moon. Perhaps you recall the classic line he uttered when he said, "That's one small step for man, one giant leap for mankind."

But let me tell you something, gang. The leap he referred to cannot hold a candle to the leap you'll be taking when the Lord comes in the clouds to rapture His Church.

"Wait a minute," you say. "I have a problem with this because I don't see the word 'rapture' in the Bible."

That's because you're using the wrong Bible! You see, the New Testament was written in Greek, and the phrase in verse 17 translated, "caught up," is the Greek word harpazo, which means, "to be grabbed by the collar and taken up with force." When the New Testament was translated into Latin, translators used the word raptus for harpazo, from which we get our word "rapture."

What are the purposes for the Rapture? I have four suggestions.

To Take Up God's Children

Before World War II, Japan and Germany called their ambassadors away from America and back to their respective home countries. So too, before the Lord declares war on the sin of our planet, He will take us, His ambassadors, home (II Corinthians 5:20).

You can't pick up a newspaper or turn on a TV without agreeing that the world is in a terrible state and needs to be judged definitely and decisively. But before God judges our Christ-rejecting, sinful world, He will take His kids home to Heaven.

If my house was infected with termites and I had to fumigate, even if my kids were being a bit rebellious or difficult, I would still make sure they were out of the house before the tent went up and the gas pumped in. Therefore, if we earthly parents are concerned about our children's safety, how much more is our heavenly Father concerned about the safety of His children?

To Shake Up the Heathen

Not only will the Rapture ensure our safety, but it will also bring about salvation. Preaching on the day of Pentecost, Peter spoke of the day when the sun shall be darkened, when the moon shall be turned to blood, and when those who call upon the name of the Lord shall be saved (Acts 2:16-21).

There are family members who have listened to you share Jesus, but they don't believe on Him. There are friends who have heard your testimony and say, "That's all well and good—for you." There are co-workers with whom you've shared the plan of salvation who seem only to turn a deaf ear. But the day is coming when we will be taken up suddenly, and all your words to those with whom you've shared will make perfect sense.

"Well, if that's the case," you say, "I'll just wait until you guys disappear. Then I'll know what you said is true, and I'll receive Jesus as my Savior."

But if you cannot receive Jesus Christ in this day of grace, what makes you think you will be able to stand for Him in that time of intense persecution? Yes, those who acknowledge Jesus as Lord during the great Tribulation will be saved, but they'll lose their heads in the process (Revelation 20:4).

Lifesaving techniques dictate that if a drowning person fights against him, a lifeguard must knock out the drowning person in order to save him. So too, the Tribulation is God's knockout punch to shake up the heathen in order to save them.

To Wake Up a Nation

In referring to the Tribulation as Jacob's trouble (Jeremiah 30:7), Jeremiah makes it clear that it has a specific purpose for the nation of Israel. After rejecting the Messiah when He walked among her, Israel will at last recognize Him during the Tribulation.

> When thou art in tribulation, and all these things are come upon thee, even in the latter days, if thou turn to the LORD thy God, and shalt be obedient unto his voice; (For the LORD thy God is a merciful God;) he will not forsake thee, neither destroy thee, nor forget the covenant of thy fathers which he sware unto them.
>
> *Deuteronomy 4:30*

How will this come about?

The two witnesses, whom I believe to be Elijah and Moses, will preach in the streets of Jerusalem (Revelation 11). One hundred forty-four thousand Jewish Billy Grahams will preach throughout the world (Revelation 7). Angels will preach in the skies (Revelation 14).

And when Jesus returns with ten thousand of His saints, all of Israel will lift up their eyes and say, "Where did You get those wounds?"

"In the house of My friends," He will answer (see Zechariah 13:6).

"And so all Israel shall be saved...." (Romans 11:26; see also Romans 9:6-8 and Galatians 6:16)—"Jews for Jesus" in totality! What a glorious day that will be!

To Make Up the Millennium

At creation, God covered the earth with a blanket of water which filtered out the ultraviolet rays (Psalm 104:6). That is why Adam, Methuselah, Enoch, and the boys lived nine hundred years or more. It was a perfect, wonderful environment. But when the world became so evil in the days of Noah that God had to flood it by breaking the protective water canopy, man's lifespan went from nine hundred years to only seventy years.

The Tribulation will purge the world of the depravity which permeates our planet to such a degree that in the Millennium, even ecology will be restored. That is why the mountains shall break forth into song and the trees of the field shall clap their hands (Isaiah 55:12), why the wolf will lie down with the lamb (Isaiah 11:6), and why men will live as long as they did in the days of Genesis (Isaiah 65:20).

As the funeral procession made its way through the streets of Nain, Jesus had compassion on the bereaved mother. "Do not weep," He told her. Then, although it would have rendered Him ceremonially unclean, Jesus touched the coffin and said to the young man inside, "Arise" (see Luke 7:11-15).

Gang, the day is coming when, as He did to the young man, Jesus will say to us, "Arise! Come up here" (see I Thessalonians 4:16). And up we'll go.

"Oh, but my heart is so hard," you say. "I'm a believer, but my heart is like stone."

It couldn't be harder than the heart of the young man in the coffin—he was dead! But that didn't prevent him from rising and speaking at the sound of Jesus' voice. If you're a believer, you will not be left behind. Your heart will be softened, your lips will flow with praise, and you will be free.

But maybe your heart is not heavy, maybe it's broken. The broken-hearted mother of Nain lost her only son. But the ultimate, only Son, Jesus Christ, showed compassion to her.

In Hawaii recently, a man said to me, "Jon, I'm so sorry you lost your daughter."

I had to say, "You know what? I didn't lose her. I know right where she is. And I will see her again."

You who are broken-hearted, be comforted. Like the widow of Nain, if you're missing a loved one, rejoice. You will soon be reunited forever.

Jesus is coming, and He will call us to be with Him. Comfort each other with these words, gang. Keep talking about His coming. Keep looking for His coming, for whether we're hard-hearted or heavy-hearted, His coming is the ultimate answer to every heart problem.

But ye, brethren, be not weary in well doing.

II Thessalonians 3:13

Chapter Eight

Be Not Weary in Well-Doing

Sometimes we grow weary in serving, in giving, in sharing, and in ministering. But here, at the end of Paul's teaching concerning the Second Coming of Christ and the establishment of His Kingdom, the Holy Spirit inspires Paul to give the Thessalonians a short exhortation with long-term implications.

Why were the Thessalonians not to be weary in well-doing? Let's look at Numbers 7 where we find the following...

It came to pass on the day that Moses had fully set up the tabernacle and had anointed it, that the princes of Israel, heads of the house of their fathers, who were princes over the tribes, brought their offerings before the Lord. And he that offered his offering on the first day was Nahshon, the son of Amminadab, of the tribe of Judah. And his offering was:

> One silver charger, the weight thereof was an hundred and thirty shekels, one silver bowl of seventy shekels, after the shekel of the sanctuary; both of them were full of fine flour mingled with oil for a meat offering; one spoon of ten shekels of gold, full of incense; one young bullock, one ram, one lamb of the first year, for a burnt offering; one kid of the goats for a sin offering; and for a sacrifice of peace offerings, two oxen, five rams, five he goats, five lambs of the first year.

On the second day, Nethaneel, the son of Zuar, prince of Issachar, did offer:

> One silver charger, the weight whereof was an hundred and thirty shekels, one silver bowl of seventy shekels, after the shekel of the sanctuary; both of them full of fine flour mingled with oil for a meat offering; one spoon of gold of ten shekels, full of incense; one young bullock, one ram, one lamb of the first year, for a burnt offering; one kid of the goats for a sin offering; and for a sacrifice of peace offerings, two oxen, five rams, five he goats, five lambs of the first year.

On the third day, Eliab, the son of Helon, prince of the children of Zebulun, did offer:

> One silver charger, the weight whereof was an hundred and thirty shekels, one silver bowl of seventy shekels, after the shekel of the sanctuary; both of them full of fine flour mingled with oil for a meat offering; one golden spoon of ten shekels, full of incense; one young bullock, one ram, one lamb of the first year, for a burnt offering; one kid of the goats for a sin offering; and for a sacrifice of peace offerings, two oxen, five rams, five he goats, five lambs of the first year.

On the fourth day, Elizur, the son of Shedeur, prince of the children of Reuben, did offer:

> One silver charger of the weight of an hundred and thirty shekels, one silver bowl of seventy shekels, after the shekel of the sanctuary; both of them full of fine flour mingled with oil for a meat offering; one

golden spoon of ten shekels, full of incense; one young bullock, one ram, one lamb of the first year, for a burnt offering; one kid of the goats for a sin offering; and for a sacrifice of peace offerings, two oxen, five rams, five he goats, five lambs of the first year.

On the fifth day, Shelumiel, the son of Zurishaddai, prince of the children of Simeon, did offer:

One silver charger, the weight whereof was an hundred and thirty shekels, one silver bowl of seventy shekels, after the shekel of the sanctuary; both of them full of fine flour mingled with oil for a meat offering; one golden spoon of ten shekels, full of incense; one young bullock, one ram, one lamb of the first year, for a burnt offering; one kid of the goats for a sin offering; and for a sacrifice of peace offerings, two oxen, five rams, five he goats, five lambs of the first year.

On the sixth day, Eliasaph, the son of Deuel, prince of the children of Gad, did offer:

One silver charger of the weight of an hundred and thirty shekels, a silver bowl of seventy shekels, after the shekel of the sanctuary; both of them full of fine flour mingled with oil for a meat offering; one golden spoon of ten shekels, full of incense; one young bullock, one ram, one lamb of the first year, for a burnt offering; one kid of the goats for a sin offering; and for a sacrifice of peace offerings, two oxen, five rams, five he goats, five lambs of the first year.

On the seventh day, Elishama, the son of Ammihud, prince of the children of Ephraim, offered:

> One silver charger, the weight whereof was an hundred and thirty shekels, one silver bowl of seventy shekels, after the shekel of the sanctuary; both of them full of fine flour mingled with oil for a meat offering; one golden spoon of ten shekels, full of incense; one young bullock, one ram, one lamb of the first year, for a burnt offering; one kid of the goats for a sin offering; and for a sacrifice of peace offerings, two oxen, five rams, five he goats, five lambs of the first year.

On the eighth day, offered Gamaliel, the son of Pedahzur, prince of the children of Manasseh:

> One silver charger of the weight of an hundred and thirty shekels, one silver bowl of seventy shekels, after the shekel of the sanctuary; both of them full of fine flour mingled with oil for a meat offering; one golden spoon of ten shekels, full of incense; one young bullock, one ram, one lamb of the first year, for a burnt offering; one kid of the goats for a sin offering; and for a sacrifice of peace offerings, two oxen, five rams, five he goats, five lambs of the first year.

On the ninth day, Abidan, son of Gideoni, prince of the children of Benjamin, offered:

> One silver charger, the weight whereof was an hundred and thirty shekels, one silver bowl of seventy shekels, after the shekel of the sanctuary; both of them full of fine flour mingled with oil for a meat offering; one

golden spoon of ten shekels, full of incense; one young bullock, one ram, one lamb of the first year, for a burnt offering; one kid of the goats for a sin offering; and for a sacrifice of peace offerings, two oxen, five rams, five he goats, five lambs of the first year.

On the tenth day, Ahiezer, son of Ammishaddai, prince of the children of Dan, offered:

One silver charger, the weight whereof was an hundred and thirty shekels, one silver bowl of seventy shekels, after the shekel of the sanctuary; both of them full of fine flour mingled with oil for a meat offering; one golden spoon of ten shekels, full of incense; one young bullock, one ram, one lamb of the first year, for a burnt offering; one kid of the goats for a sin offering; and for a sacrifice of peace offerings, two oxen, five rams, five he goats, five lambs of the first year.

On the eleventh day Pagiel, the son of Ocran, prince of the children of Asher, offered:

One silver charger, the weight whereof was an hundred and thirty shekels, one silver bowl of seventy shekels, after the shekel of the sanctuary; both of them full of fine flour mingled with oil for a meat offering; one golden spoon of ten shekels, full of incense; one young bullock, one ram, one lamb of the first year, for a burnt offering; one kid of the goats for a sin offering; and for a sacrifice of peace offerings, two oxen, five rams, five he goats, five lambs of the first year.

On the twelfth day, Ahira, the son of Enan, prince of the children of Naphtali, offered:

> One silver charger, the weight whereof was an hundred and thirty shekels, one silver bowl of seventy shekels, after the shekel of the sanctuary; both of them full of fine flour mingled with oil for a meat offering; one golden spoon of ten shekels, full of incense; one young bullock, one ram, one lamb of the first year, for a burnt offering; one kid of the goats for a sin offering; and for a sacrifice of peace offerings, two oxen, five rams, five he goats, five lambs of the first year.

The longest chapter in the Bible is Psalm 119, wherein the Word is portrayed as a teacher, a comforter, a lamp unto our feet, a light unto our path. Extolling the power and beauty of the Scriptures, Psalm 119 is worthy of its length.

But Numbers 7—the second longest chapter in the Bible—seems, at first reading, redundant, repetitive, and rather like a waste of time. The Bible is God's instruction manual for how to live. Why, then, does He seemingly waste paragraph after paragraph in chapters like Numbers 7, recording the gifts brought to the Temple? Couldn't the Lord have simply said all of the princes gave exactly the same offering, and used the leftover space to talk about things that really matter, things like marriage or child-rearing? Why does He list the offerings one at a time?

The author of Hebrews gives us the answer:

> For God is not unrighteous to forget your work and labour of love, which ye had

shewed toward his name, in that ye have ministered to the saints, and do minister.

Hebrews 6:10

In Numbers 7 and similar passages, God is saying, "I delight in individually listing what each one of these men has done for Me. Although it might be boring to you, it delights Me to record for all eternity the gifts each of My children has given Me. It doesn't bother Me a bit to take space in My Word to record what each man gave. To you, it might seem repetitive and redundant. To me, it's delightful and important. I will not forget."

Consequently, dear brothers and sisters, whatever you give, whatever you share in the Name of the Lord, will not be forgotten. Others may not see what you've given or the sacrifices you have made in time and energy. But the Lord sees. And He who sees in secret will reward you openly (Matthew 6:4).

If you are giving, loving, and sharing without any recognition, without anyone knowing, the Lord is delightfully, happily, and accurately recording your labor of love in eternity. He will not forget any good work you do—even if it is nothing more than giving a child a cup of cold water (Matthew 10:42). Don't be weary in well-doing!

"I have a problem with this exhortation," you may be thinking, "because I don't care about rewards in Heaven. I'd rather be rewarded now. I'd rather use my time and energy for my own recreation, my own pleasure. I don't care about treasures in Heaven. I want treasures now."

When you see the Lord and He opens the books to determine what rewards He will be able to heap upon you, your heart will leap for joy if He finds your page full of sharing, giving, serving, and teaching. But if your page is empty, your heart will break.

"Wait a minute," you say. "I thought there were no tears in Heaven."

According to Revelation 7:17, God shall wipe away every tear—which some have suggested to mean that there will be tears in Heaven. If this be the case, I believe those tears will come on the day we stand before our Lord and give an account of all the blessings He heaped upon us, all the abilities He gave to us, all the opportunities He opened before us which we wasted because we grew weary in well-doing.

Think of it this way...

All year long, we give financial contributions to this group; we help with that project; we donate to this ministry; we help fill that need—perhaps all the while saying, "Ouch, this hurts." But on April 14th, it all changes to "Whew! I'm glad I gave to that one. Oh boy, I'm glad I shared with this one," as we see how our donations positively affect our tax return.

So too in Heaven. Right now, we might be struggling, sometimes growing weary in well-doing. But when we get to Heaven, it's April 14th because then we'll say, "Wow, Lord, I can't believe the rewards I receive simply because of the little service I did for You. I only wish I would have done more."

Brethren, be not weary in well-doing. Make sure you're investing in eternity with your time, money, abilities, and energy. God remembers, rewards, and takes delight in everything You do for Him.

Who being the brightness of his glory, and the express image of his person, and upholding all things by the word of his power, when he had by himself purged our sins, sat down on the right hand of the Majesty on high.

Hebrews 1:3

Chapter Nine

Heaven Ain't that Far Away

The central message of the Book of Hebrews is, "Consider Jesus." At the outset, the author tells us why He came, when in verse 2 of chapter 1, he explains that Jesus is God's final Word. Then, in the second half of verse 2 and on into verse 3, we see who He is through seven characteristics of the Incomparable Christ.

In the text before us, the author continues to consider Jesus...

Where He Is

> ...When he had by himself purged our sins, sat down on the right hand of the Majesty on high....
>
> *Hebrews 1:3*

If you were in the sandals of the Hebrew Christians to whom this book was written, this statement would be shocking, even scandalous.

Why?

Because the priests in the Tabernacle and later on in the Temple never sat down. If you went into either place, you would see the brass altar, the huge laver, the table of showbread, the altar of incense, the golden candlestick, and the ark of the covenant—but not a single chair because the work of a priest was never done. You see, the sacrifices made by the priests could never take away sin. That's why they had to be offered again and again. Yet this Man, Jesus, the High Priest, sits down.

Why?

Because when He cried "IT IS FINISHED" from the Cross, it meant the work was done. Thus, when He went into Heaven, He sat down—not out of exhaustion, nor out of frustration, but out of complete and total relaxation—knowing the price had been paid for all of Jon Courson's sins—past, present, and future.

What He's Doing

Wherefore he is able also to save them to the uttermost that come unto God by him, seeing he ever liveth to make intercession for them.

Hebrews 7:25

What's our great High Priest doing? He's talking to the Father about your situation. Think with me about the intercessory ministry of Jesus...

Only hours away from His crucifixion, looking at Peter, Jesus said, "Simon, Satan has desired to sift you like wheat. But I have prayed for you, and when you get through this trial, strengthen the brothers" (see Luke 22:31-32). In other words, "Satan desires to rip you apart, to wipe you out, to do you in, but I have prayed for you, and when you get through—and you will get through—help others."

In Philippians 1:6, the promise is given to us that He who has begun a good work in us will continue to perform it until the end. It's a done deal. Jesus is not pacing. He's sitting in Heaven, talking over your situation with the Father with complete confidence that He will see you through ultimately, completely, and totally. That's His ministry...

There I am at what used to be Candlestick Park. The San Francisco 49ers are playing the Dallas Cowboys. It's a close game. The battle has been brutal. The score has seesawed back and forth. With time running out in the fourth quarter, the 49ers are trailing by six. There's sixty yards to go to score. Steve Young calls the play, sets the team down, takes the snap, and drops back.

Deep, deep goes Jerry Rice, and running alongside him, step-for-step, is 'Neon' Deion Sanders. Rice runs a perfect post-pattern. He breaks away, but Sanders catches up. The ball is in the air. It's a beautiful pass. Both men go up for it, and both have their hands on it. They come down, and it looks like Jerry Rice has it. But what's this? We can't believe what we're seeing as a little red flag comes out of the hip pocket of the referee.

We stand to our feet in anxiety. Who's it against? The referee makes the call against Sanders! The 49ers win!

Later on that evening, Tammy and I watch highlights of the game on CNN. I see Steve Young's pass. I see Sanders and Rice both go for it. I see Rice come down, the flag drop, yet I am totally at rest.

Why?

Because I know the outcome.

So does our Lord. He knows how it's all going to come out. He promises to see us through. He will complete that which He has begun. That's why He can say, "When you make it through, strengthen others."

He's seated at the right hand of the Father—but He's

not always seated...

Stephen starts preaching about the reality of Jesus Christ. What happens? The crowd becomes so incensed that people start throwing rocks at him. And as the stones begin to strike him, he says, "I see Heaven opening and the Son of God standing" (see Acts 7:56).

I would have thought it would have been just the opposite. I would have thought Jesus would stand as we go through life. Then, when we finally get to Heaven, He would say, "Whew. You made it. I can sit down now." But, as is true in all areas of spiritual life, Jesus does just the opposite of what I would do. He's sitting down when we're going through life because He's sure we're going to make it. But when we get to Heaven, He stands up to welcome us, saying, "Enter into My joy!"

Here's the challenge for me. I tend to think, "Well, somewhere way up there beyond the blue, the Lord is sitting at the right hand of the Father, thinking about me, interceding for me."

I suggest to you that nothing could be further from the truth. Think with me...

Scientists have been telling us for a number of years that atoms are composed primarily of space. In fact, if I were to squeeze out all the space between the nucleus of the atoms and the electrons which circle them within your own body, you would be reduced to the size of a speck of dust. That's why scientists say it is theoretically very possible that there could be an entirely different material world in this place right now which we can't see or hear. In other words, a tree could be growing through the roof of the sanctuary right now if the space of its atoms coincided with the solid part of the atoms of everything we see. Theoretically, then, due to the fact that if a single atom in Jacksonville, Oregon, was enlarged to the size of a basketball, its electron, proportionately, would be in Philadelphia, and there would be ample space for people, trains, planes, even armies to pass through our midst unnoticed.

What does this have to do with the ministry of Jesus, with Him praying for me, with Him being seated at God's right hand? Everything. You see, Jesus said something radical when He stated that the kingdom of God is among you (Luke 17:21). The word translated "among" is entos in Greek—a word referring to location. Thus, Jesus said the kingdom of God is not out there beyond the blue. It's among you right here, right now.

"But Jon," you protest, "haven't you always taught that when the Rapture comes, Jesus will come in the clouds?"

Yes, but I suggest that we are looking at clouds in the wrong way. Hebrews 12:1 says we are surrounded by a cloud of witnesses. Who are these witnesses? Hebrews 11 identifies them as Abraham, Moses, Samson, Gideon, and Jephthah—the heroes of the faith. So perhaps when Jesus comes, it won't be in a nimbus or a cumulus cloud. It will be, as Jude says, with ten thousand saints, in a cloud of witnesses. Where are these witnesses right now? They're not "out there." They're right here. Ask Gehazi...

"Master, we're in trouble," he cried. "The Syrians are surrounding our city."

His master, a man of miracles named Elisha, prayed the Lord would open Gehazi's eyes. When He did, Gehazi said, "Whoa! There are angels everywhere, and they're surrounding the Syrians" (see II Kings 6:17). You see, angels were there all along. It's just that Gehazi was allowed to see a different dimension.

"That's Old Testament," you say.

Let's look at I Corinthians 11, where Paul says, "when you come together in worship meetings where the gifts are flowing, where the Body is interacting, be careful about certain issues because angels are present in the midst of the congregation" (see v. 10).

Why don't we see them?

Because they're in a different dimension. The cloud of witnesses, heroes of the faith, loved ones who have gone ahead of us are not way out there. They're surrounding us. Could it be, then, that when we die or go to be with the Lord in the event called the Rapture, we don't go somewhere way out there? Could it be that we simply step into the next dimension?

Ask Peter, James, and John. Jesus gave them a sneak preview of the coming dimension when, on the Mount of Transfiguration, they suddenly saw Elijah and Moses in their midst. Like Gehazi before them, they were allowed to see into a different dimension; they were made aware of the fact that Elijah and Moses were present, although unseen previously.

If this be true, if Heaven is just stepping into a different dimension and it's right here, what does this mean to me?

It means when I pray to my Faithful Friend, my High Priest, Jesus Christ, I'm not saying, "Hello-lo-lo. Can You hear me way up there?" No, the Lord is not somewhere way beyond the blue. He is with us always (Matthew 28:20). The kingdom of Heaven is among us. The great cloud of witnesses is presently around us. Ministering spirits are in the midst of us. Jesus Himself is in the midst of the congregation. And all of a sudden, we realize Heaven ain't that far away—not only because we'll be there soon chronologically, but because the Kingdom is surrounding us presently.

I don't see it because, like Paul, I see through a glass darkly (I Corinthians 13:12). And like Gehazi, I can't see what's going on. But I understand there is a dimension of the Kingdom round about me, and I know with certainty that the Lord is seated at the right hand of the Father, at rest, praying for me.

Nevertheless we, according to his promise, look for new heavens and a new earth, wherein dwelleth righteousness.

II Peter 3:13

Chapter Ten

Flight to Heaven

If Heaven is real, then that is all that really matters; but if Heaven is not real, then nothing really matters at all. It's all about Heaven. That's not just my conclusion. Inspired by the Spirit, Paul said, "If in this life only we have hope in Christ, we are of all men most miserable" (I Corinthians 15:19).

The passage before us deals with Heaven, even as the events of last week dealt with Heaven...

I had decided to teach on the subject of the shortness of life to the one hundred or so in attendance at Family Camp on Washington's beautiful San Juan Islands. So we joined the children of Israel on their camping journey as we looked at Exodus 12-17...

Following their release from Egypt, the first place the Lord directed the children of Israel to stop was Succoth, or "Tent Town"—a place which would have reminded them not to take this life too seriously because they were only passing through.

It was at stop number two, Etham, which means, "What Now?" that God told them He would lead them with a cloud by day and a fire by night.

Stop number three found them camped between Mount Pi-hahiroth and Migdol with their backs to the Red Sea. It was there that God said, "You might complain and wonder, question and murmur, but I will put you in whatever box you need to be in to let other people see My reality and My power" (see Exodus 14:3).

After crossing the Red Sea, the children of Israel stopped at Marah, or "Bitter," where, after drinking bitter water, they were instructed by God to throw a tree into the water—whereby it became sweet. The tree in Scripture being a picture of the Cross of Calvary, this account leads me to say, "Although the situation I'm in might seem bitter presently, I know the Lord will make it sweet eventually."

Stop number five was at Elam, where seventy palm trees and twelve wells provided an oasis for no other reason than simply to bless the children of Israel.

Stop number six led from the place of blessing to the wilderness of Sin, from which we get the word, Sinai. With nothing to eat, the children of Israel murmured and complained, until the Word—the manna—came down and fed their souls. This is a potent reminder that even when we journey through the wilderness, it's the Word, the Word, the Word which feeds our souls.

At stop number seven, Rephidim, a war broke out between the Israelites and the Amalekites. As Moses went to the mountain and held up his hands in prayer, Joshua and the Israelite solders were victorious. But when his hands became heavy, the Amalekites would gain the advantage. So, standing on either side of Moses, Aaron and Hur held up his hands, and the Israelites prevailed.

"Life is short," I said, concluding my teaching that Friday morning. "We're just passing through. We don't belong here. We're going to Heaven. And we need each other to hold up our hands along the way."

Five minutes later, we heard the news that in the early morning hours, Kelly—a wonderful brother whose smile lit up any room he entered—had taken off in his plane in order to get home before the forecasted clouds rolled in. And twenty-year-old Ryan—an incredibly gifted young man—felt compelled to accompany him. But for reasons we don't understand, the plane exploded mid-flight.

So there we sat—Kelly's widow and Ryan's parents—on the bench where I had only moments earlier concluded our time together in the Word.

Suddenly, all of the studies I had shared concerning life being short, the mystery of the Red Sea for God's sovereign purposes and plan, the clouds and the pillar of fire, experiences which could produce bitterness if we allowed them to and hands that hang down unless propped up in intercession, were no longer theoretical.

Driving home through the night with Ryan's parents, I thought, "Lord, what do I say this morning in the amphitheater to a group of people who are hurting?"

But as I opened the text, the answer was in front of me, for I realized that in the fire and explosion of the previous night, Kelly and Ryan had simply taken an early flight to Heaven.

Heaven. Peter tells us we are to look forward to Heaven. Yet the Bible doesn't really say much about it. I suggest a couple of reasons for this...

The strongest instinct in man is survival. But the beauty of Heaven can overcome and overpower even that strongest of instincts. Therefore, I believe Christians would be committing suicide to get there if Heaven were understood clearly.

I believe the second reason the Bible doesn't speak very much about Heaven is because it's impossible for us to comprehend the fifth dimension (I Corinthians 2:9).

Suppose I gave you a blank piece of paper with a dot on it. How long would it hold your attention? Maybe a second. A dot is boring because it's one-dimensional. But suppose I make it two-dimensional. Suppose I add a series of circles and lines so that it resembles the face of a man. That would be a little more interesting, but you'd still be bored with that after a short time. But what if I made it three-dimensional, not just a dot or a picture, but a statue—a Michelangelo statue of David. Although that would definitely be more intriguing, you would eventually tire of it. But how much more interesting than three dimensions is the fourth one—time and space. If you could actually talk to Michelangelo, your interaction with him would be infinitely more interesting than any picture or statue could be.

But there's a fifth dimension—a dimension we have not seen, cannot hear, and do not understand. It's called eternity, and it's going to make this life look like a dot on a piece of paper.

Paul was given a sneak preview of coming attractions. And it was after he was given a glimpse of Heaven that he declared, "For to me to live is Christ, and to die is *gain*" (Philippians 1:21, emphasis mine). This one, who had perhaps the greatest command of language in history, was left speechless in his attempt to describe what he had seen there (II Corinthians 12:4).

Therefore, on the basis of the Word of God, I promise you that Kelly and Ryan are not saying, "Is this it?" No, they're saying, "This is it!" They're not saying, "Why?" They're saying, "Wow! Truly, this is the place of righteousness—for this is the right way, the right moment, and the right place for us to be."

And when he had opened the seventh seal, there was silence in heaven about the space of half an hour.

Revelation 8:1

Chapter Eleven

The Hush of Heaven

The Apostle John is writing to a group of people who are picked on, put down, beaten up, and persecuted as they are fed to lions, crucified upside down, and ignited as candles by the hand of the Roman Emperor. As you read the Book of Revelation, keep this backdrop in mind. The temptation is to view this Book only in the context of current events and eschatology. Although current application is important, we must listen to John's heartfelt words to his audience in A.D. 96—people who had no prestige, power, or prominence—people who perhaps wondered if they even had a prayer.

"Yes! You do!" John would say resoundingly. "These winds of persecution do not have to blow you away because you do have a prayer."

> I was in the Spirit on the Lord's day....
> *Revelation 1:10*

"I was on the island of Patmos due to persecution," writes John, "but I was in the Spirit." Egenómeen en pneúmati in Greek translates literally, "I came to be in the Spirit." John wasn't saying, "I was sitting in a pew, when I suddenly found myself in the Spirit," but "I came to be in the Spirit. I actively pressed in."

How did John press in?

He prayed.

The entire Book of Revelation is a mixture of vision and prayer. And here in chapter 8, the Apostle John deals with this issue in a most powerful, picturesque, and practical way as he reminded his persecuted parishioners to pray.

According to one German church historian, the distinctive feature of early Christian prayer was the certainty of being heard. In other words, when the Early Church prayed, they believed God was actually listening.

> And when he had opened the seventh seal,
> there was silence in heaven about the space
> of half an hour.
>
> *Revelation 8:1*

Commentator after commentator will tell you the "silence in heaven" of Revelation 8:1 is a mystery. But I suggest to you our text indicates that as the prayers of the saints ascend before Him, it's as though God says, "Hush."

To the living creatures who cry Holy, Holy, Holy, He says, "Hush;" to the twenty-four elders who praise Him continually, He says, "Hush;" to the thousands of angels who serve Him perpetually, He says, "Hush;"—rendering Heaven completely and totally silent.

It's as though God says, "At this moment in time, nothing else has My attention like this prayer being offered to Me. I don't want to miss a single word."

Because our days are filled with the cacophony of noise, we don't hear each other very well. We talk, but we don't listen. We converse, but we don't understand. There is, however, one exception: two people who are totally in love can sit in a crowded, noisy restaurant and converse as though there's no one else around. And that's the idea here.

"I am passionately in love with the child speaking to Me," says God, "and I don't want to miss a word he's saying." So, like a laser, fixing His full attention on the person offering even the simplest of prayers, God listens.

People spend thousands of dollars on psychiatrists, or months waiting for a pastoral appointment when God gives His undivided, complete, and total attention to the prayers of anyone going through tribulation or trouble. The key is to pray...

> And another angel came and stood at the altar, having a golden censer; and there was given unto him much incense, that he should offer it with the prayers of all saints upon the golden altar which was before the throne.
>
> *Revelation 8:3*

The prayer which causes silence throughout Heaven is mixed with much incense. Throughout Scripture, incense speaks of intercession. Hebrews 7:25 says that Jesus Christ, our great High Priest, ever lives to make intercession for the saints. In other words, the incense of Jesus' intercession on our behalf sweetens our prayers. You see, my prayers stink because they're tainted by my flesh. I ask for something I think is good, but Jesus, knowing my request would have disastrous results says, "Father, this is how Jon is praying, but what he really means is..."

Knowing our heart, Jesus perfumes our clumsy and faulty prayers through His intercessory ministry.

> And the angel took the censer, and filled it with fire of the altar, and cast it into the earth:

and there were voices, and thunderings, and
lightnings, and an earthquake.

Revelation 8:5

The angel takes the censer of prayer, perfumed with
intercession, and casts, or literally "hurls" it back to earth.
As the answer re-enters earth's atmosphere, the whole world
is shaken with incalculable effect. John's readers, being
beat up and persecuted, are told through this prophecy
that their prayers are heard, and that, in due season, the
answer will shake their world.

And the seven angels which had the seven
trumpets prepared themselves to sound.

Revelation 8:6

What was the answer?

It was music to the ears of the persecuted, for when
these first century believers studied the Bible, they studied
the Old Testament. And when they did, they read of
trumpets...

The blast of seven trumpets preceded the collapse of the
seemingly impregnable walls of Jericho (Joshua 6:16).

The alarm of two trumpets reminded the children of
Israel that the Lord their God would bring them victory
(Numbers 10:9).

The sound of the trumpet signaled the year of Jubilee,
in which all debts were canceled and all slaves set free
(Leviticus 25:9).

Thus, the answer to their prayers was truly music to the
ears of John's congregation, for the sound of the trumpet

promised victory, liberation, and the collapse of a city even stronger than Rome.

"Interesting study," you might be thinking, "but I've been saved for a while, and I know differently. Oh, I'm not saying God doesn't listen to prayer generally, just that He doesn't hear my prayer specifically."

"My marriage was on the rocks,"

"My daughter had cancer," or

"My business was going bankrupt,"

"So I prayed and prayed and prayed, and nothing happened."

"You talk about blaring trumpets, about a fireball of an answer hurled from Heaven. That's fine theoretically, but it doesn't play that way for me personally."

If you think this way, you're not alone. Let's look at Luke 1...

> There was in the days of Herod, the king of Judaea, a certain priest named Zacharias, of the course of Abia: and his wife was of the daughters of Aaron, and her name was Elisabeth. And they were both righteous before God, walking in all the commandments and ordinances of the Lord blameless. And they had no child, because that Elisabeth was barren, and they both were now well stricken in years.
>
> *Luke 1:5-7*

Because barrenness was considered a curse, Zacharias and Elisabeth were considered sinful in the eyes of their community. Although God deemed them righteous, others believed there was a defect in their piety. This being the case, perhaps Zacharias and Elisabeth lived their lives brokenhearted, wondering what was wrong.

> And there appeared unto him an angel of the Lord standing on the right side of the altar of incense. And when Zacharias saw him, he was troubled, and fear fell upon him. But the angel said unto him, Fear not, Zacharias: for thy prayer is heard; and thy wife Elisabeth shall bear thee a son, and thou shalt call his name John.
>
> *Luke 1:11-13*

"What prayer?" Zacharias must have asked. "Prayer for a son? I stopped praying for a son thirty years ago!"

Do you understand the implication? This verse tells us that God remembers even the prayers we forget. "Give us a son," prayed Elisabeth and Zacharias. But they heard nothing day after week after month after year because God wanted to give them more than just a son. His plan was to give them the greatest man born on the face of the earth up to that time (Matthew 11:11).

Slowly I begin to understand that my prayers remain in the Lord's "To Do" box even though I may have given up hope long ago. Mixed with the sweet incense of Christ's intercession, they simmer on the altar until God answers them in a way I would never have dared dream (Ephesians 3:20).

Thus, the delay in answered prayer is not due to God's procrastination, but to His desire to exceed even our wildest imagination.

"Shhh," says God. "My child is praying."

And at the right time—maybe tomorrow, maybe next week, maybe ten years down the road, maybe half a century later—the answer will quake our world.

Every time you pray, dear saint, you have your Father's full attention. And one day,

Trumpets will sound;

Walls will fall;

Debts will be canceled; and

Victory will abound.

May God help us to be those who pray.

And I heard a voice from heaven saying unto me, Write, Blessed are the dead which die in the Lord from henceforth: Yea, saith the Spirit, that they may rest from their labours; and their works do follow them.

Revelation 14:13

Chapter Twelve

Rest In Peace

James Dobbs, a thirty-three-year-old neurosurgery resident at the University of California, San Francisco, carries a cell phone, a laptop computer, and a handheld computer organizer to stay on top of his daily schedule. He even wears a pager under his wetsuit while surfing. No wonder psychologists are seeing more and more cases of stress and fatigue caused by a syndrome which has come to be known as "information overload." After all, a single weekday edition of the New York Times contains more information than the average person in the seventeenth century would have encountered in his entire lifetime. That's why I love what Jesus stated,

> Come unto me, all ye that labour and are heavy laden, and I will give you rest. Take my yoke upon you, and learn of me; for I am meek and lowly in heart: and ye shall find rest unto your souls.
> *Matthew 11:28-29*

It is interesting to me that Jesus doesn't promise rest from a difficult relationship, rest from the pressure of a job, or rest from the expectation of a college professor. He promises rest in one's soul.

Fellow fatigued Christians, as we learn of Him, we find that the commands and demands, frustrations and expectations, the whirling and swirling of information all around us is actually redemptive. That is, it can serve a purpose.

Due to a previous commitment, Tammy and I weren't able to see one of Benny's Little League games. "How did it go, Ben?" we eagerly asked upon our return.

"Well," he answered, "before I got up to bat the first time, I went to the end of the dugout, and I got on my knees and prayed."

"That's great!" I said. "You probably parked it over the fence, huh?"

"No," he said, as a huge grin spread across his face. "I struck out. But I got to pitch the next inning!"

How often we pray, "Lord, change my husband," or "Lord, help my boss see the talent latent within me," or "Lord, let me get an A." Like Benjamin, we pray with faith and fervency—only to strike out. But there's a next inning, folks—

A big inning,

A new, big inning,

A new beginning.

It's called Heaven.

And because Jesus is preparing a place for us there (John 14:2), it is necessary that He prepare us for the place. But here's the problem: we keep getting sidetracked. God desires us to focus on the big inning, the big picture of eternity, but we remain glued to home plate—continually intrigued, interested, and tempted by the things of earth.

I'm not talking about sin necessarily, but about getting stuck in the world's trappings and priorities.

To counter this, the Lord instructed His people to put a ribbon of blue on the borders of their garments, blue in Scripture being the color of Heaven (Numbers 15:38). But over the years, people became so accustomed to seeing blue, they didn't notice it any more than you would notice someone coming in here wearing a pair of Levi's® 501® jeans.

So how does God choose to free us from the pull of the world?

Our text tells us:

> And I heard a voice from heaven saying unto me, Write, Blessed are the dead which die in the Lord from henceforth: Yea, saith the Spirit, that they may rest from their labours; and their works do follow them.
>
> *Revelation 14:13*

Who is the Lord speaking to here? To those who become believers during the Tribulation.

With the wrath of God being poured out all around them upon a Christ-rejecting, sinful world, these Tribulation saints are weary beyond anything we can imagine. And what do they hear in Heaven? "Happy are you who die in the Lord." Why? Because, at last, you will rest from your labor.

Fellow baby boomers, the older generation understood this in ways we don't, as evidenced by the inscription seen on so many headstones in generations past: Rest In Peace. Perhaps it was the hardship of their lives which made them so much more aware of the true rest awaiting them in Heaven than we are with our cars, computers, and compactors.

Our text helps me begin to understand that the gravitational pull of the world to get me to trivialize my life, to waste my time, to throw away the limited days given to me on earth to prepare for Heaven is weakened through my own personal struggles and trials, fatigue and disappointments, heartaches and tribulation. And unlike a blue ribbon that's easily forgotten or becomes an item of superstition, it is the weight of weariness or worry, sadness or stress which causes me to say, "I'm really looking forward to Heaven."

"Why do I go through this struggle year after year?" you wonder.

The reason is that it's absolutely necessary—

To get you uncoupled from the world,

To set you free from the pull of the temporal,

To get you to long for Heaven.

And I heard a voice from heaven saying unto me, Write, Blessed are the dead which die in the Lord from henceforth: Yea, saith the Spirit, that they may rest from their labours; and their works do follow them.
Revelation 14:13

If the people to whom this verse was initially written were living on an island in Hawaii, being waited on hand and foot under swaying palm trees and the setting sun, having no money problems, no physical pain, no marital stress, no child-rearing difficulties, they would probably say, "My butler should be here any minute with my filet mignon, so could You hold off Your return for a little while longer, Lord?"

Hard times will never come to an end, gang, because God knows they're the only way we'll long for Heaven and thus fix our eyes on eternity.

Jesus didn't talk about Heaven while...

Sitting on the beach,

Overlooking the ocean,

Sipping a tall glass of lemonade.

He talked about Heaven in the same passage in which He told His disciples...

One of them would betray Him,

One of them would deny Him,

And He Himself would die (John 13-14).

We don't sense the bleakness the disciples must have felt because we know the whole story. They didn't. They thought their whole lives were coming to an end. After all, they had left everything to follow this Rabbi.

Blessed are they who see...

The bigger picture,

The scope of eternity,

The kingdom of Heaven.

Jesus would say, "For they will have rest not from their problems, but in their soul."

Precious brother, dear sister, you can get on your knees every night and pray,

"God, solve this problem,"

"Take away that pain," or

"Get me out of this situation."

But it could be that those are the very things God is using to make you a man or woman who lives for Heaven.

You might pray passionately and strike out on three pitches, but never lose sight of the new, big inning just ahead.

For in one hour so great riches is come to nought. And every shipmaster, and all the company in ships, and sailors, and as many as trade by sea, stood afar off, and cried when they saw the smoke of her burning, saying, What city is like unto this great city!

Revelation 18:17-18

Chapter Thirteen

It's All Going to Burn

I am about to give you, free of charge, the best investment advice you will ever receive.

Look with me at Luke 12...

> And one of the company said unto him, Master, speak to my brother, that he divide the inheritance with me.
>
> *Luke 12:13*

Jewish tradition contained a brilliant way of dividing an inheritance. If there were two brothers, it was the responsibility of the eldest to divide the inheritance in two, and the privilege of the youngest to have first choice. This way everything was fair.

In this case, however, something went wrong, and the inheritance was not correctly divided.

> And he said unto him, Man, who made me a judge or a divider over you?
>
> *Luke 12:14*

"That's not what I'm about," answered Jesus, knowing that the real problem wasn't financial, technical, or legal. It was spiritual. The issue was not a matter of money. The issue was a matter of the heart because both brothers were covetous.

"I have heard confessions of every sin imaginable," wrote Francis of Assisi, "but I have never heard a man confess the sin of covetousness."[4]

Scripture, however, records such a confession by one who was otherwise "blameless concerning the law." In Romans 7, the Apostle Paul says the sin which damned him was covetousness.

What is covetousness?

Wanting more of that of which you already have enough.

Whether with regard to power or pleasure, clothes or cars, houses or hobbies, covetousness is any attitude which says, "Just a little more, and I'll be happy." Knowing this, Jesus said,

> Take heed, and beware of covetousness: for a man's life consisteth not in the abundance of the things which he possesseth.
>
> *Luke 12:15*

It has been rightly said that small men seek to get a little more, while great men seek to be a little more.

"I can't promise you a yacht or a big house or a Rolex or a Rolls Royce like Johnny Green could," said the young man to his girlfriend. "But I can promise you all my love."

"I love you too," answered his girlfriend, "but tell me more about Johnny Green..."

Life is not about possessions; so Jesus continued on with a parable to drive this point home...

> The ground of a certain rich man brought forth plentifully: and he thought within himself, saying, What shall I do, because I have no room where to bestow my fruits? And he said, This will I do: I will pull down my barns, and build greater; and there will I bestow all my fruits and my goods. And I will say to my soul, Soul, thou hast much goods laid up for many years; take thine ease, eat, drink, and be merry. But God said unto him, Thou fool, this night thy soul shall be required of thee: then whose shall those things be, which thou hast provided? So is he that layeth up treasure for himself, and is not rich toward God.
>
> *Luke 12:16-21*

A story was told of Dietrich Reinhold, a man known throughout his community to be very wealthy. One night he went to sleep in his huge mansion, only to wake up a couple hours later in a cold sweat, frightened by a dream in which an angel appeared to him, saying, "At midnight, the richest man in the valley shall die."

"That's me," thought Reinhold, and he sent a servant to quickly fetch the doctor.

The doctor came hastily, listened to Dietrich's story, and sat with him until the clock struck twelve. When the last bell sounded, just as Dietrich was breathing a huge sigh of relief, he heard a pounding on his door. He opened it to find one of his servants.

"Master! Master Reinhold! Hans has just died!"

And suddenly Dietrich Reinhold understood that Hans, the servant who was known throughout the region as one who loved the Lord, was the richest man in the village.

Dear friend, in one hour—and the hour could be very soon—your entire empire, however big or small it might be, could burn. In a group this size, statistics indicate that three of us will be dead before we meet in the amphitheater next season. That is why Jesus said we are fools if we're rich on earth but paupers in Heaven.

One hundred years ago, a sailor shipwrecked in the South Seas found himself washed to the shore of a small island. The natives took one look at his white skin and made him their god. "This is my lucky day!" thought the sailor. But after six months of being treated like a king and learning the customs of the people, he was shocked to discover that each god served for one year, only to be sacrificed at the end of the year to the next god.

So seeing a bigger picture than living the life of luxury for the next six months, what did this guy do? He set his subjects to work on building a boat. When it was completed five and a half months later, he got on it and sailed away.[5]

What would happen if we said, "Since Babylon is all going to burn, why don't I do something radical and spend the six months I have left to prepare for eternity? I'll use whatever I have on this earth for God's glory by giving it away or sharing it with others"? If that were truly our mindset, we'd gladly lend our little brother our new CD player or our friend our new car. You see, the problem doesn't lie with material possessions. The problem only arises when we grasp them too tightly or when they keep us from fellowshipping with our Lord or loving our neighbor.

This is a hard message to give to young people because they think they can wait to get radical until they're older. But if you're in your forties, like me, or older, you know that wrinkles and gray hair are constant reminders that life is short.

But all too often what do we do? We buy hair dye and cactus root extract from Arizona which promises to give us an extra ten minutes of life.

> And he said unto his disciples, Therefore I say unto you, Take no thought for your life, what ye shall eat; neither for the body, what ye shall put on. The life is more than meat, and the body is more than raiment.
>
> *Luke 12:22-23*

Don't make styles or health food your focus to the point that when people see you coming, they know you're going to try to get them caught up in the latest fad.

> Consider the ravens: for they neither sow nor reap; which neither have storehouse nor barn; and God feedeth them: how much more are ye better than the fowls? And which of you with taking thought can add to his stature one cubit? If ye then be not able to do that thing which is least, why take ye thought for the rest? Consider the lilies how they grow: they toil not, they spin not; and yet I say unto you, that Solomon in all his glory was not arrayed like one of these. If then God so clothe the grass, which is to day in the field, and to morrow is cast into the oven; how much more

will he clothe you, O ye of little faith? And
seek not ye what ye shall eat, or what ye shall
drink, neither be ye of doubtful mind. For all
these things do the nations of the world seek
after: and your Father knoweth that ye have
need of these things. But rather seek ye the
kingdom of God; and all these things shall be
added unto you.

Luke 12:24-31

"Consider the ravens...." This passage doesn't mean you
don't have to do anything because God will take care of you.
Even the birds know better than that. No, they do what they
can to provide for themselves, but they don't develop ulcers
in the process.

Fear not, little flock; for it is your Father's
good pleasure to give you the kingdom.

Luke 12:32

What is the Kingdom? Paul defines it not as meat or
drink, but as righteousness, peace, and joy (Romans
14:17). Righteousness, peace, and joy—these are what God
promises us if we seek first the Kingdom.

Sell that ye have, and give alms; provide
yourselves bags which wax not old, a
treasure in the heavens that faileth not,
where no thief approacheth, neither moth
corrupteth. For where your treasure is, there
will your heart be also.

Luke 12:33-34

How do we disentangle our hearts from the things of Babylon and focus on the things of Heaven? By putting our treasure there, by giving stuff away, by helping people out, by doing whatever we can to be as generous as we can possibly be. We set our hearts on Heaven not by building bigger barns, but by becoming bigger people in light of eternity.

As opposed to the current health and wealth teaching which propounds that godliness with great gain makes for contentment, Paul wrote to Timothy,

> But godliness with contentment is great gain. For we brought nothing into this world, and it is certain we can carry nothing out. And having food and raiment let us be therewith content. But they that will be rich fall into temptation and a snare, and into many foolish and hurtful lusts, which drown men in destruction and perdition.
>
> *I Timothy 6:6-9*

A Confederate spy during the Civil War, Rose O'Neal Greenhow received two thousand dollars in gold as payment for her memoirs and boarded a ship home with the gold sewn into the hem of her dress and petticoats. Sailing on the blockade-runner *Condor,* she reached the mouth of the Cape Fear River just outside Wilmington, North Carolina, when a Union ship gave chase, forcing the *Condor* aground. Rose, fearing capture and reimprisonment, persuaded the captain to send her and two companions ashore in a lifeboat; but in stormy seas, the small vessel overturned. The ship sank, and so did Rosie.[6]

Paul's right—gold can drown men. So what's the solution?

The one Paul gave to Timothy...

> Charge them that are rich in this world....
>
> *I Timothy 6:17*

I believe this verse applies to every single one of us in some respect. Why? Because having a roof over our heads, food on the table, and even a single car in our garage makes us rich indeed compared to the rest of the world.

> ...That they be not high-minded, nor trust in uncertain riches, but in the living God, who giveth us richly all things to enjoy.
>
> *I Timothy 6:17*

Don't trust in your money; don't live for it, but rather trust God who gives us all things to enjoy and live for Him.

> That they do good, that they be rich in good works, ready to distribute, willing to communicate.
>
> *I Timothy 6:18*

The word translated "communicate" literally means, "be sociable." In other words, open up your home, heart, and possessions. Give them away; let them go; be as generous as you can possibly be with everyone the Lord sends your way in any given day. The key to enjoying that which God has given us is employing it for His glory.

I join Paul in promising you that when you get to Heaven, whatever you did on earth in response to God guiding you to—

Support a ministry,

>   Give to a homeless person on the street, or

>   Share a meal with someone in need—

will not cause you to say, "Phooey. I could have built a bigger barn. Why did I give so much away?"

You'll never say that!

> Laying up in store for themselves a good foundation against the time to come, that they may lay hold on eternal life.
>
> *I Timothy 6:19*

Gang, even if the Rapture doesn't happen in our lifetime (which I am convinced it will), the riches you have generously dispensed on earth in obedience to the Spirit will make you rich in Heaven because you've been obedient to the Spirit of God.

Lay up for yourselves a good foundation.

How?

By letting go;

>   By sharing with people; and

>   By obeying the Lord.

Let us be glad and rejoice, and give honour to him: for the marriage of the Lamb is come, and his wife hath made herself ready.

Revelation 19:7

Chapter Fourteen

The Wedding Feast

June—the season of weddings! But no wedding can hold a candle to the wedding in the passage before us. Following the description of the Tribulation in Revelation chapters 6-19, we come to the Marriage Supper of the Lamb.

"Wait a minute," you say, "if the Book of Revelation does indeed flow in chronological order, since the Church is raptured in chapter 4 to begin her seven-year honeymoon with the Lord, why does the Marriage Feast not take place until chapter 19?"

The answer lies in an understanding of the Jewish marriage tradition, which comprised three stages...

The Engagement

Historically, Jewish children would often be engaged by the age of two or three—sometimes before they were even born. That is, families which shared the same values and social standing would say, "If you have a daughter and I have a son, let's agree right now that they will marry each other."

You see, the Jewish people looked at marriage as far too important to be left up to the decision-making skills of young adults. So it was up to the father specifically to arrange with other fathers to whom his son or daughter would be engaged.

Scripture records a few cases, however, when men chose their own brides. But every marriage ended in heartache or disaster...

Against his father's wishes, Esau married an Ishmaelite (Genesis 28:8-9).

Jacob fell in love with Rachel at first sight, but ended up working for her for seven years before unknowingly marrying her sister (Genesis 29).

Samson "loved a woman in the valley of Sorek, whose name was Delilah" (Judges 16:4).

Since the result of a man choosing his own wife without the directive of his father often resulted in tragedy or difficulty, it became the norm for the father to select his child's spouse.

Betrothal

The engagement led to the betrothal—usually between the ages of twelve and fifteen for a young lady. At this point, bride and groom would perhaps meet for the first time, as the father of the groom would negotiate a "mohar," or the bride price. The price would be based upon three variables:

First, it would be predicated upon the wealth and worth of the groom's father. If the father of the groom was a rich man, he would pay a high price so as not to look like a cheapskate.

Secondly, the price would be determined by the bride's worth. If she was attractive or otherwise gifted, her bride price would be higher.

Thirdly, the price was based upon the groom's work. That is, in some cases it was up to the groom to pay the price...

Because Jacob chose his own bride, he paid for her himself with seven years' labor (Genesis 29:18).

"He who marries my daughter must conquer the enemy city of Kirjath-sepher," declared Caleb. Othniel took the challenge and won (Joshua 15:16).

A Gentile named Shechem who fell in love with Jacob's daughter, Dinah, was informed her price would be the circumcision of himself and all of the men in his city as a sign of identification with the Jews (Genesis 34:15).

A portion of the bride price would go to the bride to use as security in the event she was widowed or divorced. This explains why Rachel and Leah accused their uncle Laban of "devouring their money" (see Genesis 31:15).

The remainder of the bride price went to the bride's father in compensation for the fact that, unlike a son, his daughter wouldn't be able to carry on his name, help defend him, or take over the family business.

After at least a portion of the bride price was laid upon the table, a contract would be signed to further validate the agreement. Then, the prospective bride and groom would sip from a single cup of wine, at which point they were legally betrothed.

For the following year, the couple would not drink together, drink of the vine, nor live together. The bride would begin to wear a veil, signifying that she was "taken." She would also begin to prepare her wedding dress, sometimes from material provided by the groom (Ezekiel 16:10).

Meanwhile, the groom would begin construction on what is called in Hebrew "a little mansion"—a room built onto his father's house. When the father decided the preparations were complete, his son, wearing a crown, would be sent off to his wedding (Song of Solomon 3:11).

Wedding

Although the bride didn't know the exact day of her wedding, she knew it would most likely be in autumn to allow for the completion of harvest, and that it would most likely be on a Wednesday. Wednesday was the day couples got married because Thursday was the day the courts were opened. If it was discovered on her wedding day that the bride was not a virgin, she could easily be divorced the next day.

As the preparation of her "little mansion" neared completion, the bride would begin to gather her friends to await the arrival of her groom.

On the day of his wedding, the groom and his friends—particularly his best man—would walk through the streets with trumpets blaring, taking the most circuitous route to the bride's house. Already attired in her wedding dress, when the bride heard the sounding of the trumpet, she would arise and receive a blessing from her father. Then she would run out the door to be met by the groom in the streets.

Together, they would make their way to the "huppah"—the four-postered canopy under which they would be married. The ceremony itself consisted not of vows, which were Roman and Greek in tradition, but simply a reading of the contract which had been drawn up a year before, along with a blessing.

The procession would then continue on to the "little mansion" where the best man would stand outside the door while the marriage was consummated. Why would he stand outside the door? To wait for word from the groom that the bride was a virgin—as evidenced by a blood-spotted bed-sheet. If the bride was indeed a virgin, the wedding celebration would continue for seven days. If not, the guests would go home, and the bride would face either divorce or death by stoning.

Although seven days spent in an addition to one's father's house while friends and family partied just outside the door may not sound like the ideal honeymoon to us, in the Jewish culture, being waited on for a week was glorious. You see, this would be the only time in their entire lives when the bride and groom would do no labor. Remember, there were no vacations in those days—no holiday cruises, no jets, no Maui. The one and only time people were able to kick back was during their marriage week. During this week, the bride would never be seen. The groom, on the other hand, would occasionally come out and greet the guests before bringing back food and gifts to his bride.

After seven days, the groom would present his bride to his family, friends, and community, at which time the marriage feast would begin.

Looking again at this process, it becomes a picture-perfect analogy of our Bridegroom's relationship with us...

Just as the Jewish father chose whom his child would marry, it's mind-boggling to realize that our heavenly Father elected us to be the bride for His Son (I Peter 1:2). As proof of this intent, He paid the bride price, based first upon His wealth. How rich is God? All the gold in neither the world nor the galaxies in the universe would begin to reflect His wealth. Instead, the "mohar" God paid for us was something of which He had only one: His Son (John 3:16).

Secondly, the price had to be according to the bride's worth.

I once read the story of an Arabian man who had a daughter so plain that he doubted anyone would ever want to marry her. One day, however, he received word that a man from a distant village was so taken with her that he was coming to see him with bride price in hand. Prepared to take whatever he was offered, imagine the father's surprise when the visitor offered him six cows for his daughter's hand.

"Six cows!" thought the father in amazement. "The highest price ever paid in this village has been three cows!"

So it was that the father gave his daughter's hand in marriage.

Two years later, the daughter and her husband returned to her home village where everyone was startled by her exquisite beauty.

"How is she so beautiful?" they wondered.

The answer was simple: because her husband saw her as worth six cows, a six-cow beauty is what she became.

That's how God views me. I don't understand it, but I rejoice in the fact that God looks at me and says, "I am in love with you so passionately that I'll give everything to bring you into the Kingdom in order that you might live with Me forever and ever throughout eternity." To this end, God gave not six cows or six galaxies. He gave Himself.

Thirdly, the bride price was determined by the groom's work. Jesus outdid Jacob five-fold when He labored on earth as a Man for thirty-three years. And He not only conquered a city as did Othniel, but conquered the whole world when He thrust Himself into the very heart of Hell to pay the price for my sin (Ephesians 4:9). Finally, when God became Man to identify with us in the Incarnation, it was an infinitely greater step than Shechem took to identify with the Jews, for Jesus was not only afflicted momentarily, but slain before the foundation of the world (Revelation 13:8).

The bride price paid, just as a contract was signed and a cup of wine shared by the bride and groom in a Jewish betrothal, we hold in our hands the "contract" of the Word of God, along with Jesus' promise that He would not drink of the cup again until He did so with us in the Kingdom (Matthew 26:29). And as a bride wore a veil which, although it obscured her vision, signified her relationship with the groom, so at present we see through a glass darkly, but shall one day see our Bridegroom face to face (I Corinthians 13:12).

Unlike the Jewish bride who worked for a year to fashion a garment for her wedding, there is nothing we can add to the garment given to us, as we are invited to "put on Jesus Christ" (Romans 13:14) and robe ourselves in His righteousness (Isaiah 61:10).

Like the groom who added a "little mansion" to his father's house, Jesus went to His Father's house to prepare a place for us (John 14:2). Then, at the time appointed by the Father, the Son, wearing many crowns (Revelation 19:12), will come for us, His bride (Mark 13:32). Like the Jewish bride, we don't know the day or hour of His return, but like her, we know the season (I Thessalonians 5:1). We understand the place of Israel, the problems in Jerusalem, the coming together of the European Union. We understand from Bible prophecy that the Lord's coming is near, even at the very door (Mark 13:29). Thus, like the Jewish bride, we ready ourselves for the day we will hear the trumpet and the shout (I Thessalonians 4:16), before we are caught up to meet the Lord, not on earth, but in the clouds (I Thessalonians 4:17).

In the context of a Jewish wedding, John's position as "friend of the bridegroom" (John 3:29) and his message of repentance in preparation for the coming Bridegroom (Matthew 3:3) becomes clear.

"Therein lies the problem," you say. "If the marriage is to be validated on my purity, I deserve only divorce or stoning because I sin miserably; I mess up constantly; I fail continually."

Good news! The validation of our relationship with our Bridegroom doesn't depend on our sinlessness, but on His. The vesture dipped in His blood (Revelation 19:13) is that which allows us to be presented to Him without spot or wrinkle (Ephesians 5:27).

You mean we don't have to clean up our act, do this, or do that? No, Jesus said blessed are those who are simply watching for His coming (Revelation 16:15). Blessed are those who realize the price has been paid and the work has been done.

Precious people, that's what true Christianity is—just marveling at the love of the Father and of the Son for me and for you.

Thus, we are afforded a glorious honeymoon with Him, not for seven days, but for seven years as He serves us, His bride, in Heaven (Luke 12:37). At the end of seven years, we come back to earth with Him in the Second Coming (Revelation 19:14) where, at the Marriage Feast of the Lamb, we are presented as His bride forever and ever.

And that is why we see the Marriage Feast in Revelation 19 rather than in chapter 4. The analogy is perfect.

Dear friend, if you have said, "Lord, I know I have sinned and failed, but I believe You love me and paid the price for me," rejoice! Be glad! Celebrate! In the Lord's sight, you are a six-cow woman, a beautiful, glorious bride.

And I saw a new heaven and a new earth:
for the first heaven and the first earth were
passed away; and there was no more sea.

Revelation 21:1

Chapter Fifteen

What?! No Beach?

Quite frankly, our text is a bit disconcerting, even somewhat disappointing to me. A brand new city, but no more sea? If I were creating the new Heaven and the new earth, I would have said, "There shall be no more cities and lots and lots of oceans, beaches, sand, and surf!" After all, cities aren't spoken of very favorably, even in Scripture...

The first city in the Bible was founded by a brother-hating Cain (Genesis 4:17).

The second city in the Bible was built by a God-defying Nimrod (Genesis 10:9).

The Holy City itself was filled with a prophet-killing people (Matthew 23:37).

Truly, the city is not valued in Scripture. The same is true today. When we think of the city, we think of pollution, perversion, and problems. So why does the new Heaven and the new earth consist of a city—with no beach?

In the sixties, it seemed to me like everyone in the whole country was singing "Let's Go Surfin'" along with the Beach Boys. As a sophomore at Del Mar High School, about fifty miles north of Santa Cruz, "Surf City," California, I dressed the part along with everyone else in my school: huarache sandals with tire tread bottoms, powder blue Levi's® with a block of surf wax in the left, back pocket, and a copy of *Surfer Magazine* in the right, either a red or blue and white wide-striped T-shirt, and hair parted in the middle.

Walking down the hall, a "thumbs up" sign meant we had just caught the surf report on KLIV—1260 on the AM radio dial—and Pleasure Point was breaking big.

One day in May, all decked out in my huaraches, powder blue Levi's®, etc., on my way to fifth period Spanish class, I ran into Lindsay, Chuck, and Bob going the opposite direction. "Hey, Jon," they said, "We heard it's monster stuff at Steamer Lane. We saw the Turtle in the parking lot. Let's go!"

Now, the "Turtle" to which they referred was the shortened name for the "Turquoise Turtle," my 1961 Ford Falcon—so named partly because of its color and partly because it went 0-60 in 2.5 hours.

"I can't go, guys," I said. "I've got a Spanish test."

"Come on, Jon," they pleaded. "You're the only one of us with a car."

Feeling the pressure mounting, I relented. After grabbing my lunch out of my locker, I headed out to the car with Lindsay, Chuck, and Bob—a feeling of dread beginning to wash over me. With Lindsay riding "shotgun" and Bob and Chuck in the back, I swung by their houses to get their boards. No need to get mine. My 9'6" O'Neill was always on the rack on top of my car.

Wending our way over Highway 17, Lindsay looked at me and said, "You don't look so good. You must be carsick." Little did he know it wasn't the curves in the road causing me to sweat. It was the fact that although I was a charter subscriber to *Surfer*, had a great board, and knew how to dress, unbeknownst to anyone else, I had never surfed before.

When we arrived at the Henry Cowell State Park parking lot, from which point we'd hike down to the beach and paddle out to Steamer Lane, Lindsay, Chuck, and Bob grabbed their boards. "Listen, guys," I said. "I'm not feeling so good. I'll just have my lunch and join you later."

"OK," they called over their shoulders as they ran toward the trail.

Opening my lunch, I was happy to see that my mom had packed two peanut butter, mayonnaise, and pickle sandwiches—my favorite—along with about ten homemade chocolate chip cookies, an apple, and a carton of milk. After finishing the last cookie, I knew I could stall no longer. So I trekked on down to the beach and saw Lindsay, Chuck, and Bob all doing great. Bob came in. "Come on, Jon," he said, "it's excellent out there!"

So I walked down to the water's edge, reached into the back pocket of my jams, took out my wax, and began to wax my board. Seeing Bob was looking at me rather quizzically, I realized I was waxing the wrong side. You see, I thought you were supposed to wax the bottom of the board so you could cut through the water. But I came to find out that you wax the top of the board for traction. "I'm just trying something new," I said, attempting to cover my blunder.

"Come on, Jon. Quit fooling around. Let's go," Bob said as he knee-paddled out. I followed at a safe distance—hoping he wouldn't turn around and see me paddling on my belly. (Knee paddling takes practice and coordination. I had neither.) Finally, after I had sat on my board for about half an hour, Lindsay called, "Take this one, Jon." I looked back, and sure enough, there was a beautiful swell coming right in my direction which appeared to be forty to fifty feet high. At that point, I had no other choice but to lie down and paddle for all I was worth. Then a miracle happened. I actually got to my feet and stood on my board—for about a second and a half. But being too close to the nose, I "pearled." That is, the nose of the board went underwater, causing the rest of the board to become a catapult which launched me into the air. I landed in front of the wave which proceeded to break right on top of me.

After tossing and turning underwater for what felt like forever, I finally figured out which way was up, shot towards the surface of the water for a desperately-needed gasp of air, inadvertently sucking in a huge piece of kelp in the process. Grabbing my board as it floated by, there I was— clinging to my board for dear life, with seaweed hanging out of my mouth. It was at this point that the peanut butter and pickle sandwiches began to work their way up. Suddenly, with Lindsay, Chuck, and Bob looking on in utter disbelief, I barfed on my board.

Needless to say, the entire area cleared out immediately. Although I did learn to surf later on, I was set free that day from the image I was so desperately trying to cultivate.

As this incident came to mind, I was reminded that, along with the beautiful waves, salt air, and cool breeze of the beach scene, there's also a preponderance of phoniness and jealousy, of taunting and flaunting. All kinds of things take place at the beach that we feel pressured to fit into. The same is true of the football field, basketball court, or even the business office.

Therefore, I suggest to you that one of the grand and glorious things the Lord says through our text is, "In the new Heaven and earth, I'm going to liberate you from all of the things you think appear to be so cool on the outside, but which hide a dark side underneath." You who are trapped in the business gig, the materialistic stuff, the sports scene, the Lord calls you to something bigger, something grander, something better. In the new Heaven and the new earth, the sea shall be replaced by a city.

"A city?" you say. "That's exactly where I wouldn't want to be!" Listen, those to whom John addressed the Book of Revelation were those who lived in cities. Thus, John is telling them, "Heaven doesn't eliminate your situation. It transforms it."

Gang, Heaven is not "other." It's "more." Therefore, if you want Heaven in your home, in your life, in your city, it will come not by elimination, but by transformation. If any man be in Christ, he is—not will be—a new creation. Old things are passed away. Behold all things are become new (II Corinthians 5:17).

To experience eternal, abundant life this side of Heaven, see yourself as a new creation rather than as a businessman; a child of God rather than a sports star; a follower of Jesus rather than a supermom; a fisher of men rather than an image-conscious surfer. If you do, you'll find yourself free from having to know the language, dress the part, or fit the image.

Find your identity in Jesus, fellow city-dweller, and you won't miss the beach at all. I guarantee it!

And the twelve gates were twelve pearls;
every several gate was of one pearl and the
street of the city was pure gold, as it were
transparent glass.

Revelation 21:21

Chapter Sixteen

Going Home

I've got a mansion just over the hilltop,
In that bright land where we'll never grow old;
And someday yonder, we will never more wander,
But walk on streets that are purest gold.[7]

A couple of weeks ago, on Mother's Day, I was blessed to have my mother, father, and much of our family gathered in the sanctuary of Applegate. "Mansion Over the Hilltop" was sung that particular morning, and my dad so enjoyed that song which recalled memories of his Christian upbringing in the early days. A couple of weeks later, my dad would not only be hearing that song, but experiencing its reality, for last Saturday, he suddenly went home to be with the Lord.

At the memorial service, I was reflecting with the folks gathered with our family that, my father being a bank president, streets of gold must have been an incredible sight to his eyes. But really, the idea of streets paved with gold means that those streets aren't the high point, not the most wonderful thing about Heaven—any more than streets of asphalt are here on Highway 238. Asphalt is something which is common, upon which we drive on, about which we take little thought. It is not valuable in our society. That's why we pave our streets with it. Consequently, the Lord is saying in Heaven, that which is most valuable to us in this world—gold upon which our economy is based, gold upon which wars have been fought, gold upon which men lust after—is Heaven's asphalt, meaningless and common.

Gold being equivalent to asphalt causes me to wonder what is up there of value, of beauty. The Bible says eyes haven't seen, ears haven't heard the wonderful things God has prepared for those who love Him (I Corinthians 2:9).

Gang, let me tell you something. Heaven is going to be great. The greatest thing on earth is insignificant in Heaven. Know this saints: this world is the worst it's ever going to be for you. You're going up where it's going to be a whole lot better. My dad is there. A lot of our loved ones are there as well. And this only makes our longing to go there that much more real. Where things are right, filled with indescribable beauty, Heaven is the place we're craving.

When you and I get to Heaven, we're going to say, "This is what we were looking for all along!" It wasn't Tahiti. It wasn't a better job. It wasn't a fancier car or a larger house. What we crave is the same thing Abraham craved when he looked for a city that had foundations, whose builder and maker is God (Hebrews 11:10). Abraham was looking for something solid, something real. And he knew it would not be found on this earth. So he just lived in a tent, simply, as a pilgrim, right on up into Heaven where he lives presently.

Precious people, what you're looking for is not found in the movie theater. It's not found at the mall or the sports arena. If you follow those roads, you'll find them to be tantalizingly close to the real thing. You'll think, "I'm almost happy. I've almost got it. I have my new pants and my new shirt. When I get my new shoes, I'll be set to go." But then you get your new shoes and you think, "Oh my, they're wearing out. If I had a new car to protect my new shoes, then I'd really be happy." So you get the new car and think, "This is great! I'm almost happy, but a CD player in my car would really do it for me." So you get the CD player, but your CDs don't work in your house because you don't have a CD player in your house. So you get a new CD player in order that you can play the CDs from your car to protect your shoes that match your pants that go with your shirt. And so you get a new stereo for your house—only to find out that it doesn't match the paneling on your walls. "If I could just get some new walls," you think, "then I'd be really happy." And on and on it goes.

You know what you're craving?

Heaven.

Our hearts are restless, hungering, crying out for that which is eternal. There's something in us that knows innately and instinctively that Heaven is not here. We keep looking for it, only to be greatly frustrated.

Does this mean we can't be happy until we die? No. Here's the good news: "The kingdom of Heaven is among you," Jesus declared (see Luke 17:21). This means we can experience a bit of Heaven right now if we put away the things of the world and live with the values of eternity ever before us, if we live as they do in Heaven—worshipping God. If we live for the kingdom of Heaven, life becomes a total joy here and now.

Live for Heaven now and you'll enjoy this world immensely. You'll be free in relationships. You'll be used in ministry. You'll find peace.

> The steps of a good man are ordered by the LORD: and he delighteth in his way. Though he fall, he shall not be utterly cast down: for the LORD upholdeth him with his hand.
>
> *Psalm 37:23-24*

On the day the Lord took him to Heaven, my dad, a good man indeed—a godly man of character, integrity, and strength—fell in his front yard while doing some landscaping. He went in for relatively simple knee surgery. But there were unexpected complications. This was not an accident. No, the Lord ordered it all. And though he fell physically, the Lord lifted him up, not to health through surgery, but all the way to Heaven where he is walking and leaping and praising God eternally.

These are not simply nice thoughts poetically. This is not sentimentality. It's reality.

Blessed be the God and Father of our Lord Jesus Christ, which according to his abundant mercy hath begotten us again unto a lively hope by the resurrection of Jesus Christ from the dead.

I Peter 1:3

Chapter Seventeen

A Living Hope

[Editor's Note: On March 29, 1982, Terry Courson was ushered into Heaven by way of a single-car accident. The following is the message given by Pastor Chuck Smith at her memorial service on April 1, 1982.]

I can't help but think that the world is just a little poorer today. A bright and shining light has been taken away. The world is so full of darkness. There are people who seem to bring darkness wherever they go. How desperately we need the light in these dark days. And how much we feel it when a bright light has been removed. We all feel poorer because of it. The Applegate Christian Fellowship is surely poorer today. One who contributed so much of herself, who gave so much inspiration and joy, such a vital part, having been taken away leaves that sense of loss among the entire Fellowship. And we feel poorer today because of it. Surely, the Courson family is poorer today. The spark of joy, life, and beauty that she brought to the family, to the home—it's just hard to think that she is gone. And when we think about it, we feel that sense of loss, and so much poorer. But Heaven is so much richer today.

Our loss is Heaven's gain. What a beautiful place it must be. How filled with glory and joy and light and blessing. How I long to be there, as I look around at this poor world. Death is always a time of shock—even when you're expecting it. I've stood by a bedside for weeks, waiting for the last breath, expecting it to come almost at any time. Somehow, when it does finally come, it's always a shock—even when you're expecting it. But when you're not expecting it, when it comes so swiftly and suddenly, and you're not at all prepared, it is even more of a shock. Surely, when we received the call Monday, we were so totally shocked; we were hardly able to organize our thoughts or our day. It was a day we just sort of sat in shock and could not comprehend, could not absorb what we had heard.

Death is a time of memories, memories of the past—of one we knew, one who had become a part of each of our lives. And we each remember that part she played in our own lives. The thoughts, the ideas that were shared, the hopes, the ambitions, the dreams. At times like these, all of these thoughts come racing through our minds, thoughts we have locked up in our hearts, thoughts we will cherish forever—thoughts for which we give thanks to God.

Death is always a time of questions. It causes us again to question life. What is life all about? Why are we here? What is the reason for life, it's purpose? Then there are questions about death. Why does death have to happen when it happens to whom it happens? And then there invariably come the biggest questions of all: Is this the end? Or is there life after death? Is there another dimension, another sphere where life goes on? These questions have been in the mind from the beginning of creation, questions Job wrestled with when he heard his ten children were killed in an accident. "When a man dies, does he go on living?" he cried from the brokenness of his heart. "If I could but believe this," he said, "it would be so much easier to handle the grief I'm feeling today" (see Job 14:14). But unfortunately for Job, there was no real answer—only a question.

As the age of man went on, and the age of philosophy was born, as the philosophers sought to find the answers to life and the reasons for death, they probed the possibility of life after death. Yet, even as the age of philosophy reached its zenith and was beginning to fade, the philosophers had not been able to come up with any adequate answers for man.

Then one day, in a little village called Bethany, which is on the backside of the Mount of Olives towards the Judaean wilderness away from Jerusalem, two sisters were grieving because their brother had died. And as they were grieving, word came to them that Jesus was finally approaching the village. Six days earlier, they had sent an urgent message to Him down at the Jordan River which simply said, "Come quickly. The one you love is sick." Without explanation, Jesus did not respond immediately, but stayed at the Jordan River for a couple of days after receiving this urgent message. And so by the time He made His two-day journey to Bethany, His friend had now been dead for four days. Martha, one of the two sisters, leaving those who were grieving, came out of the village on the road towards Jericho to meet Him. If you listen carefully, you can hear the bitterness and disappointment as she said, "Lord, if You had only been here, my brother would not have died" (see John 11:21).

It seems that in death, we all feel the same way. "Lord, where were You when we needed You? Lord, You could have averted the grief all of us feel today. Lord, why didn't You respond when we called for You? Lord, if only You had been here...."

"Martha, your brother will live again," Jesus said.

"Oh yes, Lord," she said, "in the last day, in the great resurrection."

"I am the Resurrection, and the Life," Jesus said. "And he that believeth on Me, though he were dead, yet shall he live. And if you live and believe in Me, you'll never die" (see John 11:25-26). Then He said, "Martha, do you believe this?" That statement is so radical that it immediately divides men into two categories—those who do believe it and those who don't, those who have eternal life and those who don't. Even as we sit here today, there are those who have hope and those who don't.

"But, there's a gross inconsistency here," you say, "because Terry lived for Jesus Christ and believed in Him with all of her heart. And yet, we have gathered for a memorial of her death."

Man defines death as the separation of soul and spirit from the body. When the EKG is flat and the heart is no longer beating, man says, "You're dead." The Bible, however, says that death is not the separation of soul and spirit from the body, but the separation of the soul and spirit from God. Therefore, if a person is living only for pleasure, he's dead even while he's still living. "He that believeth in Me shall never die," Jesus said (see John 11:26). That is, "He that believeth in Me shall never be separated from God."

The Bible teaches that the real you and me is not this body. Every day I'm more thankful for that! The body is simply an instrument God has given to me to express my true self, for the real me is spirit. What I am, what I feel, and what I think, I can relate to you through the medium of this body. By the same token, through the medium of your body, you relate to me what you are, what you feel, and what you think. And as you do, I come to understand you. I come to appreciate you, to admire you, to respect you as I come to know you. I don't know your body, I know you. The body has been the instrument by which you've been able to express yourself.

But the Bible teaches that when, through age, accident, illness, disease, or other causes, my body can no longer fulfill the purposes for which God has ordained it, when the body can no longer be an adequate medium of expressing me, when the body would give me more pain and suffering than joy and pleasure, more sorrow and grief than beauty and joy, then God in His love releases my soul and spirit from the body lest my soul and spirit would find themselves captive in a prison of pain and suffering. And as my soul and spirit leave this body, they move into another body—a building of God not made with hands, a body eternal in the heavens.

This is what Paul was telling us when he said, "For we know that when this earthly tent—that is, the body in which we presently live—is dissolved, we then have a building of God not made with hands but eternal in Heaven. So then we who are in these bodies do groan, earnestly desiring that we would move out of them—not that we would be disembodied spirits, but that we might be clothed upon with a body which is from Heaven. For we know that as long as we are at home with these bodies, we are absent from the Lord. But we would choose rather to be absent from these bodies and to be present with the Lord" (see II Corinthians 5:1-8).

The Bible teaches that, for the child of God who believes in Jesus Christ, death is only moving out of the old tent and into the beautiful new house not made with hands, but eternal in Heaven. You never think of a tent as permanent. It is always temporary. And so the contrast is between the tent which is always temporary, and the building which is eternal in Heaven.

Terry has moved out of her tent and into her mansion. "In My Father's house there are many mansions," Jesus said. "And I'm going to prepare one for you. And if I go and prepare one for you, I will come again and receive you unto Myself that where I am there you may be also" (see John

14:2-3). The Lord kept His promise to Terry. Now, shall we grieve because the Lord keeps His promises? No, we grieve because we miss her. We don't sorrow for Terry. We don't say, "Oh, poor Terry. My, what a shame." We say, "Poor us. My, what a shame. We're going to miss the input that she gave to our lives." So our sorrow is for what we have lost, not for what she has gained.

In talking of the resurrection, Paul said, "But some of you are going to say, 'How are the dead raised? And what kind of a body do they have?'" And then he goes on to answer his own question by saying, "In nature, God has taught us resurrection from the dead, for when you plant a seed in the ground, it does not come forth into a new life until it first of all dies. And then the body that does come forth out of the ground is not the body that you planted because all you planted was a bare grain" (see I Corinthians 15:35-38). In other words, as vastly different as the seed is from the flower in appearance, yet there is a definite relationship between the two.

So it is with the resurrection from the dead. I'll still be Chuck. Jon will still be Jon. Terry is still Terry—yet in a new body, "for we are planted in weakness, but we'll be raised in power; we're planted in corruption, but we'll be raised in incorruption; we're planted as a natural body, but we'll be raised as a spiritual body. For there's a natural body and a spiritual body, and even as we have borne the image of the earth and have been earthy, so shall we bear the image of the heavens" (see I Corinthians 15:42-49).

When the Lord made this tent in which we presently dwell, He not only made it out of the earth, He also made it for the earth. Our bodies are designed to exist on this planet. They're designed to withstand fourteen pounds of pressure per square inch. They're designed to take the oxygen out of this nitrogen/oxygen atmosphere of ours. They're not designed for the moon. They're not designed for any other planet in our solar system. They're designed exclusively for planet earth. When God made the body, He had the earth in mind. But it is God's purpose that my time on earth only be temporary. God has a far better plan for each of us than going on in this sick world. God plans that we be with Him in His Kingdom eternally. This body was not designed for the environmental conditions of Heaven—for whatever they may be, they are surely vastly different from those of the earth. Therefore, in desiring to bring me into His eternal Kingdom, God of necessity must take me through a metamorphosis. I have to change bodies. So this body designed for the earth will be planted in the ground. But my soul and spirit will move into that building of God not made with hands which is designed for His eternal Kingdom.

"This corruption must put on incorruption, this mortal must put on immortality," Paul declared (see I Corinthians 15:53). And then will be brought to pass the saying, "O, death, where is thy sting? O grave, where is thy victory?" It's gone through Jesus Christ because death is only a metamorphosis—a changing of body.

I watch the little caterpillar as he walks through the field. As he gets to the highway and crosses over that hot pavement, I wonder sometimes if that little caterpillar doesn't think, "Oh, I wish I could fly. I am so tired of hot, dirty feet. If I could only fly, it would be so wonderful." And he may even climb a tree, get out on a twig, and jump off, hoping to fly. But his body is not designed for flight, so he falls to the ground, still wishing he could fly. But one day, the little caterpillar will climb up the wall of your house, exude a little glue, and stick himself under your windowsill as he spins a little chrysalis around himself. In time, as you watch that chrysalis, you'll see it begin to jerk convulsively.

You'll then see it break open, and there will unfold two beautiful gold and black wings. And, perched for a moment on the chrysalis, that caterpillar, which is now a butterfly, will soon begin to fly across the yard, over the fence, and away. What happened? A metamorphosis took place, a change of body which gave the lowly caterpillar a new body designed for a totally new environment where it's feet won't be hot and dirty anymore, where it will be bound to earth no longer, where it can soar and fly.

I must confess to you, I get tired of hot, dirty feet. As I look around this world in which we live, I sometimes say, "Oh God, there is so much bitterness, so much that is wrong. I wish I could soar. I wish I could fly." But I have news for you. One of these days, I'm going to go through a metamorphosis, and I'm going to soar in God's eternal Kingdom. Why? Because Jesus said, "He who believes in Me shall never die." Today, Terry is soaring in that glorious eternal kingdom of God, where all those who love our Lord Jesus Christ are destined to be.

"Oh, thank God that we have a living hope," Peter proclaimed. How? "By the resurrection of Jesus Christ from the dead" (see I Peter 1:3). You see, Jesus told us these marvelous, exciting things—and yet we could write them all off to beautiful dreams, beautiful thoughts, nice ideas. In fact, when Jesus was nailed to the Cross, that's what at least two of the disciples did. When Jesus joined them, unrecognized, on the road to Emmaus, He said, "What's the matter? You guys look so sad."

"You must be a stranger around here if You don't know what's been going on in Jerusalem these last few days," they said.

"What things?" Jesus asked.

"Oh, there was a Man from Nazareth who went around

doing good. And we had hoped in Him for the salvation of Israel. But they crucified Him. Now it's done" (see Luke 24:13-21).

"We had hoped," they said. Their "had hoped," however, changed from the past tense to the present tense when the resurrection was realized (Luke 24:35). Theirs became a living hope by the resurrection of Jesus Christ.

And so today, we gather together and we have a living hope through Jesus Christ. We share that glorious hope today that God has given to us and confirmed by the resurrection of His Son. In a few days, the whole world will celebrate the Resurrection of Jesus Christ. And as we do, may we be reminded that the hope we have today is more than a hope. It is a living hope.

God bless you.

And after this, Abraham buried Sarah his wife in the cave of the field of Machpelah....

Genesis 23:19

Chapter Eighteen

Grief...Grave...Gift
Genesis 23

[Editor's Note: On March 29, 1982, Jon's wife, Terry, was ushered into Heaven by way of a single-car accident. The following is the message given by Jon the Sunday after her Homegoing.]

Genesis 23 is the account of the first funeral found in Scripture. It deals with Abraham, the man of faith, the friend of God, burying his beloved bride, Sarah. In it, we see Abraham's grief in verses 1-6, Sarah's grave in verses 7-9, and Ephron's gift in verses 10-20.

Abraham's Grief

Abraham and Sarah had been husband and wife for over sixty years. They had a very beautiful, very unusual relationship. In fact, the Holy Spirit inspired the Apostle Peter to record that Sarah was an example of a godly woman and that Christian sisters should seek to emulate the spirit within her (I Peter 3:6).

Sarah was a submitted sister indeed. She reverenced her husband—even to the point of calling him lord. She followed her husband even when he led her in ways that were not the best—as when, due to a famine in the land of Canaan, he took her to Egypt and actually had the audacity to have her lie on his behalf. "You're such a beautiful woman," he said, "that Pharaoh will want to take you into his harem. Just say you're my sister." Pharaoh's men did indeed come. And Sarah, saying she was Abraham's sister, was indeed taken away (Genesis 12). Yet God protected Sarah, a woman so submitted that she was willing to journey into Egypt and lay down her life for her husband, an unusual woman whom Abraham loved deeply and valued greatly.

I think of my own wife, Terry. I've led her through some very interesting experiences, taken a jaunt or two into Egypt. Yet, she was one who was submitted to me and committed to me personally. We began dating shortly before enrolling at Biola University. During the first week of school, I was pledging for a fraternity—Alpha Omega Chi. And the brothers of that fraternity made us do all sorts of unusual things. We had to carry around a cardboard box and a broom to classes with us, and whenever one of the brothers in the fraternity would yell, "Air Raid!" no matter what we were doing, we had to get in our cardboard boxes and shoot down imaginary planes with our brooms. They also put eggs in our shirt and pants' pockets, which any of the active brothers in the fraternities could smash at any time.

The first day of pledging, Terry came out of her dorm dressed very beautifully, and one of the brothers in the fraternity came to me and said, "You've got to take her and throw her into the fountain right now." So, I grabbed Terry and dunked her in the fountain. She went back to her dorm, changed her clothes, did her hair up, and looked beautiful once again. As I met her outside to apologize and walk her to her next class, another brother came by and said, "Throw her in the fountain again." So I threw her in the fountain again. Over the years, I'm afraid I threw her in many, many fountains and took her many, many interesting places that she willingly went. I miss her greatly. A woman submitted to her husband is something to be prized and valued.

Brothers, if your wife has submitted to you, put up with you, and endured deep waters for you, value her.

...And Abraham came to mourn for Sarah....

Genesis 23:2

Scripture says that when Abraham came to Hebron, he mourned for Sarah. After sixty years of marriage, they were close. She was a beautiful lady. And upon Sarah's death, Abraham mourned. This is the first mention of mourning in the Scriptures. The word in Hebrew means "the beating of breasts." It's a deep-felt emotion. Throughout Scripture, we see this type of mourning related to death. We see Joseph mourning, smiting his breast for his father when Jacob died (Genesis 50:4). We see David mourning when he lost his son, Absalom (II Samuel 19:4). We see the devout men of Israel mourning over the death of Stephen (Acts 8:2). And we see Jesus mourning the death of Lazarus (John 11:35).

I did not know mourning until my present ordeal. It's in your gut. It's deep. It comes over you in waves. And it's not only something which you feel deeply, but you can't help but beat yourself for it. You see, we almost didn't go to Bend that day. We were running behind schedule, and we almost decided to go to Mount Ashland to ski instead, which we could have made quite easily. And so I think, "Was I hurrying? Was I going too fast? If I just would have... if I just..." And I have these thoughts, and it hurts. And I wonder why sometimes. "Why, Lord?" But I know it was the Lord. Of that I am confident. I know it was the Lord who took Terry home. I know statistically the chances of being in a fatal automobile accident where one person is taken immediately and the other walks out unscathed can only be explained as miraculous. I know God's hand was in it. It had to be so. Yet, I find myself with feelings which are indescribable unless you've been there. I keep waiting for the alarm clock to go off. I keep waiting for the buzzer to sound and for me to walk across my bedroom floor and knock the clock on the floor like I do each morning, and say, "Terry, I had the heaviest dream last night." But the alarm clock doesn't go off.

...And to weep for her.

Genesis 23:2

Abraham mourned for Sarah, and he wept for her as well. The word "weeping" is an entirely different word in Hebrew than the word "mourn." I find this illuminating. "Weeping" speaks of a silent, sorrowful shedding of tears. Whereas mourning is the wailing and the beating of breasts, weeping is simply the shedding of tears and the overflow of emotion from the eyes. My daughter, Jessie, is experiencing this phenomenon. She'll walk around the house with tears in her eyes, running down her little cheeks.

"Jessie, what's wrong?" I say.

"I want to die and go be with Mommy," she'll reply.

When I told five-year-old Peter and three-year-old Jessie that Terry had been taken to be with the Lord, their reactions were most interesting. Peter's was one of fascination.

"Really?" he said. "Can she fly in Heaven?"

"Yeah, Pete," I said, "she can fly."

"Is there a big hole in Heaven where she looks down and sees us right now?"

"No, Peter, there's not a hole in Heaven."

"Well, can she see us?"

"Yeah, Pete, she can see us."

"Wow, she must have good eyes."

But when I told Jessie, all she said was, "Oh, no. Oh, no. Oh, no." And her little chin quivered. Jessie walks around in that weeping state from time to time. Oh, no.

Peter's got it worked out. He said to me yesterday, "Daddy, I've got an idea. I'll die. You will hold my hand and Jessie will hold your hand and Christy will hold Jessie's hand and Kitty will hold Christy's hand. Hold on real tight, and we'll all go to Heaven." There will be a time when we will be reunited. And I told Peter that time will be soon. But it's not for right now. The Lord has things for us to do right here.

> And Abraham stood up from before his dead....
>
> *Genesis 23:3*

After mourning and after weeping, Abraham stood up from before his dead. It was time to stand up and get going again. I suppose that yesterday was the hardest day I've gone through in my entire life. I couldn't get it together emotionally. And I found myself mourning—beating myself and weeping—feeling that loss. But last night when I walked into the concert here at the Fellowship, an interesting thing took place. I was suddenly touched, strengthened, and relieved because it was time to get going again. People were getting saved. People were worshipping the Lord. The band was launching off into a new ministry.

And I speak the truth to you, I know this as a fact: the answer in the time of mourning and grief and hurt and pain is not to throw a pity party. It's to stand up and get going. The time when you're discouraged and down, the time when you're blue and defeated is the very time to stand up and start giving out, to encourage and minister to others, to pray for and bear the burdens of others. There is a time for mourning, yes, and a time for weeping. But from the deepest experience I have ever gone through, I ask you not to allow yourself to go through times when you cut yourself off from fellowship.

I didn't particularly want to go to the concert last night. But because I love Jeff, I felt a need to be there. And you know who got blessed? Me. For the first time all day, I was encouraged, lifted, built up, and strengthened. And I woke up this morning excited about life, about my Lord. Jesus said that it's in giving out that we receive. I know this to be so. I'm not talking about a theory, but about an experience. Please give out. Be faithful in ministry, in fellowship, and to each other.

>...I am a stranger and a sojourner with you....
>
> *Genesis 23:4*

Don't forget this account took place in the land given to Abraham, the land of Canaan, the Promised Land. Even in the Promised Land, which speaks of the fruitful, abundant, Spirit-filled life, Abraham said, "I'm a stranger and a sojourner. I don't belong. I'm just passing through."

When I was in the car with Terry, although I was only conscious for a few minutes before I passed out, I sensed very definitely the release of her spirit. I sensed the Lord's presence there very definitely. And although in the ambulance on the way down the mountain, they told me she was doing well, I knew in my heart that the Lord had taken her. I just knew it. And at that point, I was acutely aware of something I have been telling you for years, but which I now know: life is short. It is a vapor. It's here and it's gone. No one was more energetic or full of vitality than Terry. But we are sojourners here, strangers, and pilgrims just passing through. Therefore, living for this life is crazy. It's futile. If our goals, energy, and priorities are focused on this life, we are fools indeed. I'm aware that I'm a stranger and a sojourner in a way I have not been aware of before.

Peter-John is aware of this as well. After the Memorial Service on Thursday, I drove back to Coos Bay, where we were staying with my parents. It had been raining and hailing all day. And when I came in the door, Peter-John grabbed me and said, "Oh Daddy, me and Charlie (his cousin, also five) were praying for you. We were praying that the Lord would help it stop raining so you wouldn't die." Evidently, he connected the bad weather with the automobile accident and Terry's death. At five years of age, Peter-John is cognizant of the fact that life is a vapor. It's short, something which cannot be taken for granted or taken lightly.

> Give me a possession of a burying place with you, that I may bury my dead out of my sight.
>
> *Genesis 23:4*

In one sense, Terry will never be out of my sight. One of the most uncanny experiences I've ever had happened on Monday night, the day of the accident. I woke Peter-John at 8:30 just to see him. No one had told him that his mommy was taken. And he said, "Daddy, I'm so glad we have pictures of Mommy so we won't forget what she looks like." That stunned me and stuns me still. Somehow—I don't know to what extent—he perceived there had been a change in the family unit, and his heart was prepared.

I have pictures of Terry, not just photographs, but mental snapshots I treasure and value. But on the other hand, I understand what Abraham is saying here when he stated, "Let me bury my dead out of my sight," because something took place in death of which, again, I had no previous knowledge. That is, going into the mortuary and seeing my wife, a couple of interesting things happened. She was a beautiful lady. Yet, as she lay there, something was different in her physical make up.

My little brother Jimmy stated it perfectly when he said, "Jon, Terry is the most beautiful woman I know, but I never understood, never realized that her beauty was inward, shining outward. And now it's not the same." My brother-in-law, Larry, said it this way: "Every person in the Body of Christ has a function. Some are the hands, some the feet, some the ears. But Terry had a very special part. She was the gleam, the sparkle in the eye in the Body of Christ." Indeed there was a sparkle about Terry which enriched my life personally and many of our lives corporately. And what's been left behind, I want to bury out of my sight, not out of disrespect, but out of the realization that the inward beauty is what made Terry beautiful—the Lord Jesus Christ in her life, working through her life in a unique way.

When I went into the viewing room, for the first time in my adult Christian experience, I genuinely doubted the reality of the whole thing, and it took me back. I walked in the room and thought, "Is this whole thing real? Is she really in Heaven? Or is this just something we like to believe? Is there really a personal God? Or is it just a comforting thought to hang on to?" I really doubted. And then I beat myself for doubting. It only lasted for a few minutes, but I sat down in a chair and thought, "Why am I doubting? Why now? Why at this point in my life when I need my Lord and need to stand on the faith that God has built into my life more than any other time, why now do I doubt?"

And the Lord came and sat down beside me and gave me an interesting understanding. It's like this: if you called me and said, "Jon, I just won $1 million in the Readers Digest Sweepstakes!" I would say, "Far out! Wonderful!" I would rejoice exceedingly (and remind you to remember to tithe!). I would be so thrilled. And that's the way I always have reacted when a believer has experienced death. I've always been so confident, so excited. "Praise the Lord," I've said, "they're with Jesus right now." But if it was Terry who called me, excitedly screaming, "Jon! We've just won $1 million!" I would say to her, "Wait a minute. Calm down. Let's check it out." I would not get excited with her initially because my first reaction would be, "It's too good to be true." You see, I would want it to be true so badly that I would want to check it out first. And that's the exact thing I went through. I wanted Terry to be in Heaven so badly that I found myself going through a time of saying, "Wait a minute. Let's check this out. Let's slow it down. Let's make sure." And the Lord ministered to my heart in a way I can't explain to you.

Sarah's Grave

Sarah was buried in Hebron, which means "Fellowship." Sarah was buried in fellowship. That to me is significant. I thank the Lord that my wife was buried when she was in tight fellowship with Him. She was taken when she was ready. She was in Hebron, in fellowship. The Sunday night before the morning she was taken Home, I did something unusual during the Communion service here at church.

Because Terry helps lead worship Sunday nights, and I'm on stage overseeing the meeting, we usually aren't able to have Communion together. But Sunday night, I felt particularly impressed to share Communion with her. And the Lord met us in a very special way—one of those times I will treasure deeply in my heart forever. Then a sister came up and desired to wash Terry's feet in the foot-washing part of the meeting, and Terry was worshipping the Lord. She was ready. She was in fellowship. She was in Hebron. And I'm oh, so thankful for that. I hope you're in Hebron. I hope that if today would be the day you would be taken Home, you would be ready.

That Sunday afternoon, our conversation had drifted to the topic of heroes. "Who's your hero?" I asked her.

"Do you really want to know?" she said.

"Yeah."

"In all honesty, you're my hero. There is no one I respect more, admire more, or look up to more in the whole world than you." And she planted a kiss on my cheek. I was her hero. We were in fellowship—not fighting, not quarreling. If you're married, I hope you're in Hebron with the person you're sitting next to, because you just don't know. I hope you're in Hebron with your kids, because you don't know when your kids will be taken Home. I hope you're in Hebron with your brothers and sisters in the Lord because you just don't know but that word, that feeling, that thought you communicated to them might be the last.

> And after this, Abraham buried Sarah his
> wife in the cave of the field of Machpelah.
>
> *Genesis 23:19*

"Machpelah" means "double doors." Evidently, in this

cave there was a door in and a door out. That's exactly what death is. We only see one door—the loss. And I feel that loss. We are told that when someone has his legs amputated, for a certain amount of time, the patient still feels his toes and feet as if they were there. So too, there are times when I think Terry is in the next room. And when I realize she isn't, I feel her loss greatly. But there's another door, the door I don't see from my perspective, but through which Terry went into eternity where she's experiencing an ecstasy beyond description right now, cruising the cosmos, worshipping the Lord, feeling feelings we cannot possibly imagine. The greatest moment of ecstasy you've ever experienced in your whole life—the greatest delight, the greatest pleasure, the greatest explosion of happiness or contentment—is like taking out the garbage in Heaven. It just can't compare. Terry entered the cave of Machpelah. She went in one side, and we look at that casket and grave and think, "Oh, no."

But wait a minute. There's another door. She went out the other door. She's with the Lord. And if I didn't have that hope, I don't know what I'd do. If you're an unbeliever, I don't know how you do it, unless you choose not to think about it. But someday you will have to think about it. You will have to deal with the issue of life and death. I hope you deal with that today. I hope you don't wait until it's too late.

> The same is Hebron in the land of Canaan.
> *Genesis 23:19*

It's interesting to me that God made this fantastic promise to Abraham, saying, "Look in all directions. All the land you see will be yours." But did you know that the only part of that glorious Promised Land that Abraham ever possessed personally was this little cave of Machpelah? That was his claim to Canaan, that was the Promised Land for him. So too, as I evaluate my own life at this point in time, spiritually, where my wife is buried is my Promised Land. She's gone before me, but that's where I'm headed. This world holds even less importance to me than it did last week. And frankly, it wasn't even that important last week. My Promised Land? Machpelah—the double-doored cave.

Ephron's Gift

Ephron graciously offered Abraham his cave for free, but Abraham wanted to pay the full price for it. Scripture also says that Abraham bowed himself low to Ephron, realizing the generosity of his offer. I too have been deeply, deeply touched with Ephron's gift—with the gifts of the brothers and sisters here in the Fellowship, with the letters and the flowers, the meals and the clean house. How I appreciate that. How I'm thankful to be part of the Body of Christ. But there will come times in the future when you may offer something to me and, although I'll bow before you in gratitude, I'll just have to pay the full price. I'll just have to work it through, so I ask you to bear with me.

All I can say is that it works. The whole thing works. The Lord works. The Word works. The principles of ministry work. Praise works. The idea of a family, both physical and spiritual, works. It all works.

"Oh, Jon, you don't know. You've had an easy life." That is one accusation which will no longer be hurled at me, because if I lost one of my kids, I could still find comfort in my wife. And as much as you love your kids, they're not your spouses. Every sorrow and grief and hurt and wound I've experienced, I've always been able to share with Terry...

always. We've carried it together. But now that I'm facing the greatest wound and hurt of my entire life, I can't share it with her. And every time my little daughter Christy hops by (at one year of age, she's really into hopping), I hurt because my kids are going to miss her. But I want to tell you that even in the most painful hurts and difficulties, it works. I am in the midst of a very deep, deep trial. And it works. It really does. The Lord is faithful. The Word is solid. The Holy Spirit is a Comforter beyond description. The way of God is right. And I join with the four and twenty elders in the heavenly scene saying, "Righteous and true are Your judgments, O Lord." I don't know why. I don't know what. But I know You. And I know You're right. Jesus Christ, the solid Rock upon which I build my life, upon which I place my faith, is real. And He works.

And the peace of God, which passeth all understanding, shall keep your hearts and minds through Christ Jesus.

Philippians 4:7

Chapter Nineteen

Past Understanding

[Editor's Note: This message was given soon after the death of Jon's sixteen-year-old daughter, Jessie, in 1994.]

Here we are again, and I know a lot of us are understandably asking the question, "Why?" But for me, in the past couple of days, the question I've been thinking through is, "Why not?" I mean, the way this world is going, Jessie is the one who has it made. She's in Heaven. She's truly, absolutely, unquestionably in Heaven right now. So, why not? Why wouldn't the Lord take her?

You see, Jessie was ready. The last time I saw my daughter was on Tuesday morning, about an hour or so before she went to Heaven. She was here at the church at 6:30 in the morning for Communion. I didn't know she would be here. We hadn't met here at morning worship for probably six or eight months. "This is interesting," I thought as I watched her make her way to the Communion Table. "Here's Jessie, and here I am."

She bowed at the Table, broke the bread, took the cup, and stayed at the Table for about twenty minutes, an unusually long time. As I watched her return to her seat, I remember feeling so blessed to see my Jess beginning her day in that way, driving out here in the opposite direction of school, just to have Communion with her Lord.

At that point, Rick Vestnys, who leads morning worship, said, "If anyone feels led to pray aloud, this would be a good time to do it." And Jessie prayed, "Lord, I'm so thankful today for the promises of your Word—particularly for the promise of Jeremiah 29 where You said You know the thoughts You think towards us, thoughts of peace and not of evil, to bring us to a glorious end."

In the morning worship hour, people come and go as they wish. So after that prayer, Jessie made her way out. She walked by me, winked at me, gave me a "thumbs up," smiled, and left. I looked at Rick, Rick looked at me, and he understood that I understood that he understood the significance of what Jessie had prayed. You see, unbeknownst to her, that was the very verse I shared with you if you were here thirteen years ago when the Lord took my wife, Terry, home. Riding in the ambulance, the Lord spoke to me so powerfully; it was almost as though it was audible. "I know the thoughts I think of you," He said to my heart, "thoughts of peace and not of evil, to bring you to a glorious end." It was a verse I didn't even know I knew.

Jeremiah 29:11 is a verse that was already hugely important to me. And it became even more so when it comprised the final words I would hear my daughter speak. Rick immediately wrote a song from Jeremiah 29:11, wanting to capture that moment that meant so much to me. Then he, so sensitive to the Spirit, turned to Psalm 128 and said, "Blessed is the man that fears the Lord. His children are like olive plants around the table." Jessie had just been around the Table, and I once again appreciated the interaction of ministry taking place. Jessie walked out of the sanctuary. And I had a warmth in my heart from seeing my daughter spending time with the Lord and quoting the verse that meant so much to me.

She went back home to pick up Peter-John for breakfast, but Peter was still in bed after an exhausting basketball practice. As she walked in the door, Tammy saw Jessie and noticed she looked remarkably radiant. That's not poetic or sentimental, for when people spend time with the Lord, there's just a softness, a glow about them. "Come back here," Tammy said to Jessie. She gave Jessie a hug, they prayed together, and Jessie walked out the door. Two minutes later, she was ushered into Heaven. She was ready. The last time I saw my daughter alive was at the Lord's Table. The next time I see my daughter will be at the Lord's Table, at the Marriage Feast of the Lamb.

The last message Jessie heard me preach was on Ephesians 3:17: That Christ may dwell in your hearts by faith. I ended the study, saying, "When Jesus is comfortable in your heart, when He has access and entry into every room, He'll say, 'Thank you for letting Me dwell in your house. But I have a better house. Let's go there instead.' And when the time is right, He'll take you to Heaven. But that's another story, a story I can't tell because I haven't been there. The Bible tells us that eyes have not seen nor ears heard the things the Lord has prepared for those who love Him." My daughter chose to finish the sermon for me. Christ was indeed comfortably at home in her heart. He's chosen to take her to His home. And she is elated.

Jessie opened her heart to Jesus when she was three years old. She came to me one evening after family devotions and said, "Daddy, I want Jesus to live in me."

"OK," I said. "Let's pray."

So she prayed to receive Jesus as her Savior. And she walked with Him. Jessie never rebelled, she never questioned her faith, and she never got sucked into the world. To our knowledge, she never went through one day when she questioned or doubted her faith in any way. She just walked with the Lord.

In fact, I remember when she was four years old, on a camping trip with Peter-John, Christy, and I, she said, "Daddy, why is that man smoking?"

"Oh, it's just something some people do," I said.

"Well, it's not right," she said. And before I could stop her, she marched over to the man and said, "If you smoke on earth, you'll burn in Hell."

Unfortunately, I couldn't get there fast enough to put out the fire! Jessie's theology wasn't exactly right, but her zeal was radical.

Later on that summer, on another camping trip, noticing some men decked out in waders fishing on the bank of the river, Jessie said, "Daddy, I want to go fishing."

"Jess," I said, "we don't have any fishing poles."

Jessie, being one to always make things happen one way or another, searched along the bank of the river until she found a stick. "Daddy, I got a pole," she said.

"Jessie, you need line and a hook. And we just don't have those."

But again, after searching near the fishermen, she found eight feet of line with a rusty hook at the end. "Daddy," she said, "I found some line and a hook."

"Jessie," I said, "you can't just fish with a line and a hook on a stick. You need bait."

"Oh," she said. And she marched over to the fishermen with their waders and high-tech equipment, pulled on the vest of one of them, and said, "Could I have some bait?"

"They're not biting anything today, honey," he said.

"But I need some bait," Jessie insisted.

"OK," he said, and gave her a salmon egg.

So I put the line on the stick and the egg on the hook, and Jessie proudly took her place beside the fishermen. They didn't catch a thing. Jessie, however, wasn't there for five minutes before she pulled out a trout—a little trout, but a trout nonetheless.

That's the kind of girl Jessie was. By hook or crook, she'd make things happen. And it used to intrigue and fascinate us. Spiritually, she became a very effective fisher of men.

In the past week, the letters sent to us from people Jessie encouraged to walk with Jesus have astounded us. Among them, the following...

> I am writing to you to tell you I'm sorry for the loss of a family member. I know saying I'm sorry won't bring Jessie back. But I want you to know I miss Jessie with all of my heart. She and I weren't best friends, but she and I were good friends. She put me back on the road to Heaven. I was walking the wrong road, and on the way up to the Spiritual Life retreat my freshman year, Jessie and I got on the subject of Heaven.
>
> I said, "How do you feel about Heaven?"
>
> And she said, "I'm ready to go right now." Then she said, "How about you?"
>
> And I said, "No, I've been in a Christian family all my life, but I've decided to do my own thing."
>
> We started talking, and I decided right then that Christianity was the way. Jessie helped me when I was down. She was like my spiritual

mother. I want you to know I will miss her as long as I live. I know that the way I feel about her death is not anything like you feel because I was not related to her. But I still suffer from a huge loss. John 15:13 says, "Greater love has no man than this, that one would lay down his life for his friends." I know Jessica would do this for anyone in the world—even for her enemies. Satan thinks he's won a big victory by us losing such a warrior for God. But really, he has lost in the long run because about ninety percent of the people of this school are so much stronger now. So Peter and Christy, I want to be accountable to you now that your sister is gone. Please help me and hold me accountable. And I will pray for your family.

We have stacks of letters like this from kids and adults who were touched by my little fisher of men. But in addition to hearing about Jessie's work evangelistically, there's something else that intrigues me. As a Bible teacher, simply going through her Bible in the last couple of days has profoundly impacted me. Her Bible is one I gave her a few months ago. She wanted one just like mine (before my eyes went bad!). So I got her this one, a Cambridge Cameo. The notes are amazing. But that shouldn't totally surprise me. You see, Rick and I were holding a retreat on the mountaintop a few months ago, teaching on the Book of Revelation. Jessie loved to come to the retreats, and she was there for the weekend. I ended one session by saying, "Take an hour on your own to ponder and consider the things we've looked at in Scriptures. Then we'll meet again and share together."

So half an hour later, the folks came back, and Jessie said, "I'd like to share."

"OK," I said.

"I've been considering the seven bowl judgments at the end of the Tribulation period," she said. "And I've noticed that they correlate perfectly to the seven sayings of Christ from the Cross." And she went on to chronologically match each judgment with each saying. Then she made the application, saying, "Either we will embrace what Jesus did for us in going through tribulation and anguish for us on the Cross, or we will have to be recipients of the bowl judgments."

The correlation was one I had never even begun to consider. Rick and I looked at each other, and thought we should quit the ministry right there, retire, and let Jessie take over. She was an unusual young lady. In my estimation, she was a finished product.

Someone asked me, "But why did the Lord take her so young?" I was able to respond, "Yes, she was young, but she's never going to have wrinkles, cancer, or marital difficulties."

Monday evening before she went to Bible study, the day before she was taken to Heaven, Ben and Mary were out with friends, and Peter was working. So it was just Tammy, Jessie, Christy, and me sitting at the table. Somehow, we got on the subject of dating. And I said, "Jessie, you are so sharp, your love for the Lord is so real, and your knowledge of Him is so deep that you will have a real challenge in waiting for someone who will be able to truly lead you and not be mothered by you. You need to wait until that guy comes on the scene."

When the girls left, Tammy and I talked further, realizing that this was no small order. But the next morning, she found the One I know will truly lead her, the One who is the perfect Bridegroom for her.

I was telling someone recently that one of the things I was most looking forward to was officiating at my daughter's wedding. And in a very real sense, this is a marriage ceremony. Sure, there are tears. There always are at weddings. But my daughter has the best Bridegroom in the history of the cosmos. Right before this service began, Rick came to me and said, "We found Jessie's ring that was lost in the accident." And he gave it to me. It was her Cascade High School class ring. And I thought, "That's terrific. This really is a marriage ceremony." Jessie is truly the Bride of Christ. She's in Heaven. She's with Jesus.

Quite frankly, although I appreciate the love and sympathy and tears of so many, it is I who should be crying for you who have daughters not yet married because life is hard. I'm the one who married my daughter off to the Perfect Bridegroom—One who will never fail her in any way. There will never be a cross word. There will never be a horrible fight. Therefore, I feel in one sense, I'm the luckiest father tonight because my daughter is safely deposited in Heaven. And, by her own admission, she was ready to go.

Jesus told us that wherever a man's treasure is, there will his heart be also. My family has a significant investment in Heaven. And it just makes Heaven all the more dear to us. The world is fading away; the world is falling apart. But the greatest thing a dad can feel is that his children are safely deposited in Heaven. Then his own heart is inclined even more in that direction.

Some might say, "So she's in Heaven. So she has the perfect Bridegroom. But she was only sixteen years old. There are some good things she'll miss out on." And I wouldn't argue that point except to say this: The best experience, the most ecstatic feeling this world has to offer is equivalent to taking the garbage out in comparison to what transpires in

Heaven. How do I know? Because the streets in Heaven are paved with gold. In other words, that which the world fights and dies for is mere asphalt in Heaven.

"But won't she miss her family and friends?" some ask. Peter tells us that one day is with the Lord as a thousand years, and a thousand years as one day (II Peter 3:8). Now, if a thousand years are as a day, one hundred years would only be about two and a half hours. Therefore, even if we lived to be one hundred years old, Jessie would only have to wait for us a couple hours. And she can wait that long.

But the second part of that verse is also true—that a day is as a thousand years. Taking my family over to the Coast the day Jessie was taken to Heaven was a day that seemed to me to last a thousand years. There was a storm in Bandon. And the pounding rain pelted the little hotel we stayed in. As I sat in one of the rooms with my older kids while Tammy tended the younger ones, time dragged. We all just wept and wept and wept. And I must admit to you that on the Coast, my faith was shaken.

I didn't have any idea that I would be at this place in these circumstances again. And as I sat there and thought and tried to pray, that day, for me, was as a thousand years.

I looked out the window and thought of what happened almost thirteen years ago on the same Coast after their mother had been taken to Heaven in the same way with the very same injury as Jessie. While Nana took care of Christy, I walked on the beach with Peter-John and Jessie and told them their mommy had been taken to Heaven. Five years old at the time, Peter-John was intrigued. "Can she see us? Can she fly? Can she cut a hole in the floor of Heaven and look down and watch us?" he asked.

Answering his questions as well as I could, I looked

over at three-year-old Jessie, and saw great big tears rolling down her chubby cheeks. All she could say was, "Oh, no. Oh, no. Oh, no." And I scooped her up and held her tight.

And as I looked out over the same ocean thirteen years later, I heard my heart echoing Jessie's, "Oh, no. Oh, no. Oh, no."

That night, and for the two following, Tammy sobbed convulsively in her sleep.

The next morning, I grabbed my Bible, but nothing seemed to minister. Then suddenly, a certain passage of Scripture was brought to life for me. And the Lord met me again.

He keeps doing that. He keeps honoring what He told us is true—that if we draw near to Him, He'll draw near to us. And as my Bible was getting soaked both from the storm and from my tears, I found myself remembering what I learned last time around. Sitting on the couch a few days after Terry went to Heaven, I said, "Why Lord?"

And the Lord spoke to my heart in a way which is so important. He said, "My Word has promised you a peace that passes understanding. Have you experienced that?"

"Yes, Lord," I said. "I do have peace. It's inexplicable."

"All right then," He said, "Never seek a peace that comes *from* understanding. I'll always give you a peace that *passes* understanding."

And how right the Lord is because if He gave me a peace that comes from understanding, from intellect, or from logic, I would argue with Him.

"Did You ever considering accomplishing the same thing another way?" I would ask. "Did You have to do it this way?"

So He says, "I'm going to bypass your brain and give you a peace in your heart instead."

Truly, we can drown in the oceans of "Why?" But this I do know: When I have question marks—as I have had this week—they're turned into exclamation marks when I draw near to Him. The "Oh, no's" are turned into "I know!"

I know what? I know Whom I have believed and am persuaded that He is able. When my questions well up, I realize Romans 5 says that God demonstrated His love for me in that when I was a sinner, Christ died in place of me. Jesus died on the Cross. And that is the Cross-Examination that answers every question ultimately.

"Jon, you sound so preacher-ish," you might be thinking.

You know why? Because Peter-John nailed it. He came in a few days ago and said, "Dad, it works. When you're facing things you thought you could never go through, it works."

And at the risk of being thought of as in shock or callused, I must tell you that Peter-John is absolutely right. It works. Faith works. Jesus works. He's there for us in the time of tragedy and difficulty. He meets you at that point in a way you never thought you could be met. And the insights that are gained, the understanding gleaned in the thousand years we go through in the day of doubt and despair, are like what happened to Joshua the day the sun stood still. The day was elongated in order that the enemy might be defeated and the Promised Land taken.

Jessie's prayer was heard and it's true. For her, for Tammy, for me, for Peter-John and Christy, Mary and Benjamin, it's true. He knows the thoughts He thinks towards us, thoughts of peace and not of evil to bring us all to a glorious end.

And he shewed me a pure river of water of life, clear as crystal, proceeding out of the throne of God and of the Lamb. In the midst of the street of it, and on either side of the river, was there the tree of life, which bare twelve manner of fruits, and yielded her fruit every month: and the leaves of the tree were for the healing of the nations.

Revelation 22:1-2

Chapter Twenty

A Place for You

[Editor's Note: This message was given at the memorial of Jon's dad, Merle Courson, in 1992.]

On Saturday, our dad's heart stopped suddenly and unexpectedly. And when we heard the news, our hearts skipped a beat—or two or three—and then they broke in agony. But as the day unfolded, we experienced something. We discovered again the reality of the words of Jesus Christ, the One who has shown such amazing grace to our family. We discovered the reality of the words He spoke to His followers, to His family, before He was to leave them when He said, "Let not your hearts be troubled"—your hearts that have skipped a beat, or two or three, your hearts which have broken in agony. "Let not your hearts be troubled." He would say to you and to me, "You believe in God, believe also in Me. In My Father's house are many mansions: if it were not so, I would have told you. I go to prepare a place for you" (see John 14:1-2).

That's the fact. That's the truth. "I go to prepare a place for you," Jesus said. And what a place it must be. The word "Heaven" appears 557 times in the Bible. Yet, although it's mentioned frequently, the descriptions are rather sketchy. Why isn't Heaven described more clearly?

The Bible says, "Eye hath not seen, nor ear heard, neither have entered into the heart of man, the things which God hath prepared for them that love him" (I Corinthians 2:9). It's indescribable, this place called Heaven. After all, how could you describe to a man born blind the brilliant colors of a sunset? How could you describe to a man born deaf what Beethoven's Ninth Symphony sounds like? It can't be done.

So too, God cannot describe Heaven to us very vividly because it's beyond our wildest imaginations. It's a place beyond description. And that's our hope today. We come missing our dad deeply, but celebrating the fact that he is in Heaven, in a place beyond description.

I look around and see the creative genius of God—at the mountains and at the coast. All over, we see His spectacular creative abilities. But He created all the wonders that we see in six days. Over two thousand years ago, Jesus said, "I am going to prepare a place for you." Therefore, if He made all we can see in six days, imagine what He could do in two thousand years' time! It must be absolutely mind-boggling!

A couple of days ago, Tammy took four-year-old Benjamin and his four-year-old cousin, David, to the dump in Jacksonville. "Uh-oh," Benny said as he got out of the car. "Somebody littered." "It wasn't me, Aunt Tammy, honest!" little David was quick to respond.

Truly, the things we'll see will make the finest things on earth look like the Jacksonville dump in comparison. In fact, the Bible says the streets there are paved with gold (Revelation 21:21). People think gold-paved streets must be wonderful—especially in the eyes of a bank president like my dad. But in reality, golden streets are not the highlight of Heaven. Not at all. We pave our streets with asphalt. We drive over it. We walk across it. We take no notice of it. So what the Lord is saying to us by telling us the streets in Heaven are paved with gold is simply that the most valuable commodity on earth—that upon which our economy is built, that for which wars have been fought, that for which men have died—is like asphalt in Heaven. We won't even notice it because of the wonderful things we'll see and experience.

But please understand, our Lord said, "Don't let your hearts be troubled," not because of the beauty of Heaven in totality, but because, "I go to prepare a place for you personally, for you specifically." Therefore, if the Lord has prepared a place for my dad specifically, I know that place must be landscaped beautifully...

Every Saturday, as I was growing up in Campbell, California, out would come the old push mower. Dad always liked to mow the lawn himself because he could do it just right, making the lines on the freshly cut grass perfectly parallel. But almost without fail, somewhere between the side yard and the apricot trees in the front, he would stop and say to my brother Jimmy and me, "Let's play some Horse." We'd grab a basketball and go to the driveway, where we'd shoot baskets and play a game of Horse—or two or three. He would always win.

He'd always have time for us before finishing the yard and creating a thing of beauty. That's why I know that when we see Dad's mansion in Heaven, it will be landscaped beautifully. And I bet he will even get to mow the lawn, where he'll do it just right.

It's not only my earthly father who loves gardening, but my heavenly Father does as well. When He created the first man, it was in a garden that He placed him. And we are told in the Book of Genesis that Adam walked with God in the garden in the cool of the day. The Last Adam, as the Scriptures call Jesus, was also One who spent time in gardens. He talked to the Father in the Garden of Gethsemane, where Luke tells us He went frequently.

It was in a garden that the first Adam walked with the Father, and it was in a garden that the Last Adam talked to the Father. I find this interesting because my mom shared with me a couple of days ago that my dad was rising before the dawn broke to walk out to the orchard to garden before leaving for the bank. "It's where I can talk to God as I'm tending the trees or watering the lawn," he had told her. So, like the first Adam, my dad walked with his Father in the garden. In one of the few descriptions of Heaven we are given in the Bible, we read of a crystal river, of a garden-like setting, of trees whose leaves are used for healing. And I believe my dad is there right now.

It's not only my dad who can walk with God in the garden, who can talk to God in the garden, so can you and so can we, for "whosoever will..." can come freely.

> And the Spirit and the bride say, Come. And let him that heareth say, Come. And let him that is athirst come. And whosoever will, let him take the water of life freely.
>
> *Revelation 22:17*

Live for Heaven now and you'll enjoy this world immensely. You'll be free in relationships. You'll be used in ministry. You'll find peace.

> Thank You, Lord, that because of what You did on Calvary, our sins will not keep us from living forever with You in a place that's right. We have seen the stupidity and futility of this world, the emptiness, the short pleasures of sin that lead to destruction. But You've saved us from that and given us the promise of eternal life with You in a place where every tear shall be wiped away, every

question answered, every wrong righted.
How we look forward to that time, Lord. How
we look forward to being with You forever.
How we look forward to Heaven.

Chapter Twenty-One

Last Words

> Behold, what manner of love the Father hath
> bestowed upon us, that we should be called
> the sons of God...Beloved, now are we the
> sons of God, and it doth not yet appear what
> we shall be: but we know that, when he shall
> appear, we shall be like him; for we shall see
> him as he is. And every man that hath this
> hope in him purifieth himself, even as he is
> pure.
>
> *I John 3:1-3*

Perhaps as you've read this book, you've come to realize that you are not a son of God, you are not a Christian. Heaven sounds like a wonderful place—and it is—but you are not sure you're going there. Good news! You can have that assurance today. How? By believing in and receiving *the* Son of God—Jesus Christ.

> But as many as received him, to them gave
> he power to become the sons of God, even to
> them that believe on his name.
>
> *John 1:12*

Jesus said that we "must be born again" (John 3:7). What does it mean to be born again? Simply this: recognizing that you are spiritually bankrupt before God and in need of a new birth.

You see, man was originally created to live in fellowship with God. That fellowship was broken when Adam, the first man, disobeyed God's command by taking that first bite of the forbidden fruit. He was in essence telling God, "You will not rule over me! I am going to be master of my own destiny." When Adam rebelled, he died, not physically, but spiritually because God had said, "In the day that you eat of it, you shall surely die" (see Genesis 2:17). The relationship that Adam and Eve had enjoyed with the Lord was broken, and they were cast out of the garden.

Move forward two thousand plus years...

Jesus, speaking to the multitudes in Capernaum, said: "He that comes to Me, I will in no wise cast out" (see John 6:37). How could Jesus say that? Because He saw another garden—the Garden of Gethsemane—that place where He would pray to the Father three times, "If there is any other way man can be forgiven, let this cup pass from Me, nevertheless, not My will, but Thine be done" (see Matthew 26:39).

What is the cup to which Jesus refers? The cup of suffering—separation from His Father for you and for me. When Jesus died on the Cross, He died for the sins of the world. All the bad things you've done, all the sins I've committed, all the ugliness of mankind was placed on the shoulders of our Lord, and this caused the Father to turn away from His Beloved Son. The fellowship that they experienced from the beginning of time was broken.

> And about the ninth hour Jesus cried with a
> loud voice, saying, Eli, Eli, lama sabachthani?
> that is to say, My God, my God, why hast
> thou forsaken me?
>
> *Matthew 27:46*

Matthew goes on to say that Jesus, after He had cried out once more, "yielded up the ghost." He died. "What?!" you might ask. "Jesus, the Son of God, the One who claimed to be Messiah, the One who raised others from the dead is gone? How can that be?" The disciples and those who followed Him were asking the same questions. They were devastated, dejected, and depressed!

But wait. The story doesn't end there. Jesus told the disciples earlier that He would die, but He also told them He would rise from the dead!

> The Son of man must be delivered into the hands of sinful men, and be crucified, *and the third day rise again.*
>
> *Luke 24:7, emphasis mine*

Three days later, Jesus, the Perfect Man, the Creator of the universe, and the Giver of life defied death by rising again!

What does this mean for us? Another Gospel writer records this statement of Jesus from the Cross:

> "It is finished!" And bowing His head, He gave up His spirit
>
> *John 19:30, NKJV*

This glorious statement, "It is finished," can be literally translated "paid in full." The penalty for our sin has been paid! And the Resurrection was the Father's stamp of approval on that payment.

> Him [Jesus] hath God exalted with his right hand to be a Prince and a Saviour....
>
> *Acts 5:31*

He [the Son] humbled himself, and became obedient unto death, even the death of the cross. Wherefore God [the Father] also hath highly exalted him, and given him a name which is above every name: That at the name of Jesus every knee should bow, of things in heaven, and things in earth, and things under the earth; And that every tongue should confess that Jesus Christ is Lord, to the glory of God the Father.

Philippians 2:8-11

At the name of Jesus, *every knee shall bow!* That statement fills my heart with joy! Why? Because I have already bowed my knee to Him and confessed Him as my Lord. Have you? You see, you can either bow before Him *today*, or you will be made to bow before Him on *that day*—the day when He will judge the whole world. You will either enjoy fellowship with the Father for eternity, or you will be separated from the Father eternally.

Remember, Heaven isn't some far off place where angels fly about and we play harps while sitting on white, fluffy clouds. Heaven is Jesus!

Consider once more the end of the story—the Book of Revelation:

And I John saw the holy city, new Jerusalem, coming down from God out of heaven, prepared as a bride adorned for her husband. And I heard a great voice out of heaven saying, Behold, the tabernacle of God is with men, and he will dwell with them, and they shall be his people, and God himself shall be with them, and be their God.

Revelation 21:2-3

And I saw no temple therein: for the Lord God Almighty and the Lamb are the temple of it. And the city had no need of the sun, neither of the moon, to shine in it: for the glory of God did lighten it, and the Lamb is the light thereof.

Revelation 21:22-23

How can you be sure you're going to Heaven?

...That if you confess with your mouth the Lord Jesus and believe in your heart that God has raised Him from the dead, you will be saved. For with the heart one believes unto righteousness, and with the mouth confession is made unto salvation.

Romans 10:9-10, NKJV

Confess Jesus as your Lord today, and you will have that assurance, based on the very Word of God itself, that you will be saved.

So why not talk to the Lord right now and invite Him into your heart? Simply pray something like this:

Lord, I know I've messed up...I've sinned. But if it's true that You died in my place to pay the price for my sins, and You really did rise again, then Lord, I invite You right now into my heart to be my Savior and to take control of my life, both now and forevermore. I believe in You, and I desire Your Lordship in my life. So thank You, Jesus, for coming into my heart and for giving me a fresh start this very moment. I'm Yours, Lord! In Jesus Name. Amen.

If you've prayed that prayer, welcome to the family of God! My encouragement to you now is to "purify yourself just as He is pure" (see I John 3:3). How? By following the example of the Early Church:

> And they continued stedfastly in the apostles' doctrine and fellowship, and in breaking of bread, and in prayers.
>
> *Acts 2:42*

1. *The apostles' doctrine*: Stay in the Word—read your Bible.

> Sanctify them through thy truth: thy word is truth.
>
> *John 17:17*

> That he might sanctify and cleanse it with the washing of water by the word, That he might present it to himself a glorious church, not having spot, or wrinkle, or any such thing; but that it should be holy and without blemish.
>
> *Ephesians 5:26-27*

2. *Fellowship*: Find a Bible-believing, Bible-teaching church or Bible study in your area.

> And let us consider one another in order to stir up love and good works, not forsaking the assembling of ourselves together, as is the manner of some, but exhorting one another, and so much the more as you see the Day approaching.
>
> *Hebrews 10:24-25, NKJV*

3. Breaking of bread: Communion is important because it celebrates our Lord's death. However, it is also a tangible reminder of our need for cleansing.

> For as often as you eat this bread and drink this cup, you proclaim the Lord's death till He comes. Therefore whoever eats this bread or drinks this cup of the Lord in an unworthy manner will be guilty of the body and blood of the Lord. But let a man examine himself, and so let him eat of the bread and drink of the cup. For he who eats and drinks in an unworthy manner eats and drinks judgment to himself, not discerning the Lord's body. For this reason many are weak and sick among you, and many sleep. For if we would judge ourselves, we would not be judged. But when we are judged, we are chastened by the Lord, that we may not be condemned with the world.
>
> *I Corinthians 11:26-32, NKJV*

Whenever we come to the Table and examine ourselves openly before the Lord, He is always faithful to show us those areas that are hindering us in our fellowship with Him.

4. Prayers: In the Scriptures, we see Jesus speaking to the Father often. In the same way, prayer has been given to us so that we might communicate with our Father. But the Bible also declares that our prayers are a sweet-smelling incense before the Lord. When we pray, we are blessing our Father in Heaven.

> And the smoke of the incense, which came
> with the prayers of the saints, ascended up
> before God out of the angel's hand.
>
> *Revelation 8:4*

One other thing that we see prevalent in the Early Church was witnessing—those first Christians loved to share the Gospel! Now that you've been born again, go tell someone about Jesus.

And then someday, on a day not too far away, we'll all be together in that Glorious Place which He is presently preparing for you, for me, and for those people we shared with and prayed for who became part of His forever Family.

When we're there, we'll have all eternity to share our stories with each other of how our loving Lord rescued us from the pit and brought us into His presence. And then we'll worship Him together with passion...Ah, that will be Heavenly!

It's really going to happen. I guarantee. You watch, you wait, you'll see!

Endnotes

[1] Source unknown.

[2] C.S. Lewis. *Mere Christianity.* Harper Collins, 2001, pgs. 136-137.

[3] Source unknown.

[4] Source unknown.

[5] Source unknown.

[6] Source: "Historical Times Encyclopedia of the Civil War" edited by Patricia L. Faust.

[7] Ira Stamphill, "Mansion Over the Hilltop." 1949.